Great Short Poems
from Antiquity to the
Twentieth Century

DOVER · THRIFT · EDITIONS

Great Short Poems
from Antiquity to the
Twentieth Century

EDITED BY
DOROTHY BELLE POLLACK

❧

DOVER PUBLICATIONS, INC.
Mineola, New York

DOVER THRIFT EDITIONS

GENERAL EDITOR: MARY CAROLYN WALDREP
EDITOR OF THIS VOLUME: BOB BLAISDELL

ACKNOWLEDGMENTS: see page xxiii.

The publisher gratefully acknowledges the generous assistance of Bob Blaisdell in the preparation and selection of poems for this volume.

Copyright

Bibliographical Note

Great Short Poems from Antiquity to the Twentieth Century is a new compilation, first published by Dover Publications, Inc., in 2011. Unless otherwise noted, new translations of poems have been made for this edition by Dorothy Belle Pollack from the French, Latin, Greek, and German.

Library of Congress Cataloging-in-Publication Data

Great short poems from antiquity to the twentieth century/
edited by Dorothy Belle Pollack.
p. cm.—(Dover thrift editions)
Includes index.
ISBN-13: 978-0-486-47876-0
ISBN-10: 0-486-47876-9
1. Poetry—Collections. 2. Poetry—Translations into English.
I. Pollack, Dorothy Belle.
PN6101.G73 2011
808.81—dc22

2010047936

Manufactured in the United States by Courier Corporation
47876901
www.doverpublications.com

~

Introduction

~

"Poetry is the music of the soul," said Voltaire. How well he captured the very essence of poetry in that one short phrase!

From time immemorial, humankind has meditated on the nature of our universe, recording those meditations for later ages to ponder and enjoy. Included here are more than 300 poems—all brief—for your reading pleasure. They were written by 190 different poets, representing countries all over the globe.

Our poets span the time from ancient Greece and Rome right down to the twentieth century, from Archias to Yevtushenko, from Anacreon to Yeats, they come from totally disparate backgrounds. They have different styles of writing; they use different verse forms. The poems have been arranged alphabetically by the poet's name within each of the five sections.

But the key word is "brief." Most of the poems here are 12 lines or under. They take but a moment to read, but in that moment, you will surely reap wisdom and delight.

You will be amazed at the multiple themes these writers have chosen: love, beauty, nature, art, mourning, myth, brotherhood, war, peace, mortality, and the list goes on and on. Many writers are famous worldwide; some are less well-known, but nonetheless gifted.

Life always has its serious and humorous moments, and our poems reflect this.

Persia's Sadi and China's Su T'ung-Po make us think. America's Aldrich makes us smile, and England's Belloc makes us laugh outright.

Some of these poets, like Sappho, Hitomaro, and Heine, have put their sad lives into their poetry, and we sigh at the thought of their suffering. Some, like Morley, slyly comment on human foibles, and we recognize ourselves! Still others, like Baudelaire and Kafka, shock us, by questioning our accepted truths.

Emerson thought we should begin each day by reading a poem—not a bad idea. In fact, you may even find yourself memorizing some of the lines herein.

We hope these poems will bring you as much pleasure, as we have experienced in gathering them.

Poetry will always have a universal appeal, for, as William Carlos Williams observed, "The province of the poem is the world."

—DOROTHY BELLE POLLACK

Contents

∿

Acknowledgments

Robert Creeley: "After Lorca" from *The Collected Poems of Robert Creeley*, 1975. Reproduced with permission from The University of California Press via Copyright Clearance Center.

Martín Espada: "Confessions of the Tenant in Apt. #2" from *Trumpets from the Islands of their Eviction* by Martín Espada; Bilingual Press/Editorial Bilingüe, 1987, 1994, Tempe, Arizona. Reprinted by Permission of Bilingual Press/Editorial Bilingüe.

Langston Hughes: "Personal" from *The Collected Poems of Langston Hughes* by Langston Hughes, edited by Arnold Rampersad with David Roessel, Associate Editor, copyright © 1994 by the Estate of Langston Hughes. Used by permission of Alfred A. Knopf, a division of Random House, Inc.

D. H. Lawrence: "Change" from *The Complete Poems of D. H. Lawrence* by D.H. Lawrence, edited by V. de Sola Pinto & F. W. Roberts, copyright © 1964, 1971 by Angelo Ravalgi and C.M. Weekley, Executors of the Estate of Frieda Lawrence Ravalgi. Used by permission of Viking Penguin, a division of Penguin Group (USA) Inc.

Marianne Moore: "I May, I Might, I Must," copyright © 1959 by Marianne Moore, © renewed 1987 by Lawrence E. Brinn and Louise Crane, Executors of the Estate of Marianne Moore, from *The Complete Poems of Marianne Moore* by Marianne Moore. Used by permission of Viking Penguin, a division of Penguin Group (USA) Inc.

Christopher Morley: "Prudence" by Christopher Morley, from *Translations from the Chinese* (1927), Doubleday, Page & Co. Reprinted with permission from the Estate of Christopher Morley, through its Executor, Mr. John Christopher Woodruff.

Dorothy Parker: "Sweet Violets" from *Dorothy Parker: Complete Poems* by Dorothy Parker, copyright © 1999 by The National Association for the Advancement of Colored People. Used by permission of Penguin, a division of Penguin Group (USA) Inc.

Theodore Roethke: "Heard in a Violent Ward," copyright © 1964 by Beatrice Roethke, Administratrix of the Estate of Theodore Roethke, from *Collected Poems of Theodore Roethke* by Theodore Roethke. Used by permission of Doubleday, a division of Random House, Inc.

Gertrude Stein: "I am Rose" from *The World Is Round* by Gertrude Stein. Reprinted with permission from the Estate of Gertrude Stein, through its Literary Executor, Mr. Stanford Gann, Jr., of Levin & Gann, P.A.

Dylan Thomas: "The Hand That Signed the Paper" by Dylan Thomas, from *The Poems of Dylan Thomas*, copyright © 1939 by New Directions Publishing Corp. Reprinted by permission of New Directions Publishing Corp.

Yevgeny Yevtushenko: "Knock at the Door" by Yevgeny Yevtushenko, from *Poems Chosen by the Author* (1971). Peter Levi and Robin Milner-Gulland, translators. Reprinted by permission of Robin Milner-Gulland.

"Poets are the unacknowledged legislators of the world."
—PERCY BYSSHE SHELLEY (1792–1822)

Antiquity

~

Note: All poems in this section have been translated by Dorothy Belle Pollack.

ANACREON
(570 B.C.–488 B.C.)

Nature's Laws

Earth drinks up brook,
And then the tree
Drinks up the earth.
In turn the sea
Drinks rivers up.
And so 'tis done.
Sun drinks up sea,
And moon the sun.
Well then, my friends,
Don't make outcry;
If all do drink,
Why shouldn't I?

This Is My Lifestyle

The wealth of Gyges, Lydian king,
   To me will never matter.
Gold will not contentment bring,
   And tyrants I will not flatter.

I much prefer to scent my hair,
   And wreathe my head with roses.
This day is my concern and care,
   Not what the next discloses!

ANONYMOUS

Ancient Roman Lullaby

Lullaby, my little chap;
Either take your milk or take your nap.

Old Roman Prayer Against the Gout

I remember you, spirits.
Do please cure my feet.
   Keep plague from the land;
   Let health be at hand;
Watch my feet, I entreat!

AUSONIUS
(c. 310 A.D.–395 A.D.)

The Spartan Mother

The Spartan mother, arming her son with his shield,
Said unto him—"WITH or UPON THIS, return from the field."

BIBLE (OLD TESTAMENT)

Psalm 15

Lord, who shall sojourn in Thy tabernacle?
Who shall dwell upon Thy holy mountain?
He that walketh uprightly, and worketh righteousness,
And speaketh truth in his heart;
That hath no slander upon his tongue,
Nor doeth evil to his fellow,
Nor taketh on a reproach against his neighbour;
In whose eyes a vile person is despised,
But he honoureth them that fear the lord;
He that sweareth to his own hurt, and changeth not;
He that putteth not out his money on interest,
Nor taketh a bribe against the innocent.
He that doeth these things shall never be moved.

CALLICTER

The Patient's Epitaph

Phidon didn't purge
Or touch me; all the same,
Feeling ill of fever,
I but recalled his name—
　　　　And died.

CATULLUS
(c. 84 B.C.–c. 54 B.C.)

Vivámus (Let us live!)

Come let us live, my Lesbia,
And love, and count for aught
The talk of those severe old men
With criticism fraught.
Suns can set and then return
Once more unto our sight,
But ere our brief light fails, we must
Sleep through a lasting night.
A thousand kisses give me; add
A hundred more, and then,
Another thousand, hundred, with
A thousand more again.
When many thousands we shall give,
We shall confuse the count,
Lest we two know, or anyone,
Divining their amount,
Cast evil eye on this
Our one true source of bliss.

My Lesbia and I

Lesbia scorns me so,
You'd think that she abhors me.
But may I die right now,
If Lesbia doesn't adore me.
And how do I know 'tis true?
The signs are the same with me:—
I scorn her all the time,
Yet love her fervently.

But does she speak true?

My love says no one will she wed
    In all the land
But me, were Jupiter himself
    To seek her hand;
But still a woman's words unto
    Her anxious love
Should be inscribed on rapid streams
    Or winds above.

I Cannot Stop from Loving You

My mind's been led to such a state
By you, my Lesbia, of late,
That I can't give respect or praise,
Though you should try to change your ways.
Nor can I stop from loving you,
No matter what you ever do.

Odi et Amo (I Love and Hate)

I love and hate; you ask perhaps
    How this can be.
I know not, but I feel the pain
    Is deep in me.

CLAUDIANUS
(370 A.D.–410 A.D.)

Double Trouble

A dreadful poverty
And Cupid cruel oppress me.
Starvation I can bear,
But the pangs of love distress me.

DIONYSIUS CATO
(fl. 4th century, A.D.)

Work

Work of ten dries our tears; 'tis true.
And work is a source of blessings too.

Time Tells

Wrongs may be hidden out of sight;
But remember, in time, they come to light.

Men's Ways

In talk men's ways are revealed,
And sometimes, too, concealed.

ENNIUS
(239 B.C.–169 B.C.)

His Epitaph

The bust, oh citizens,
Of Ennius behold.
Your fathers' greatest deeds
With fervor he retold.

Let none bewail my death;
Let none shed tears for me.
Alive, upon men's lips,
I'll flit eternally.

HADRIAN
(76 A.D.–138 A.D.)

The Emperor Hadrian Addresses His Soul

My little soul,
My gently wandering soul,
Of my body the friend and guest,
Where do you now depart?
What regions grim and dark,
Recessed,
Do you seek?
And will you no longer jest
With me, as you were wont to do
With zest?

HERACLITUS
(early 5th century, B.C.)

"You may travel far and wide"

You may travel far and wide
But never will you find
The boundaries of
The soul.

HOMER
(c. 9th century, B.C.)

Alike Unto Leaves

Alike unto leaves is the race of men,
The leaves which the wind to the ground doth strew.
But the season of spring arrives, and then
The burgeoning woodland blooms anew.

So the races of men is born and dies.
These things learn well, that you may know
What many others do surmise
Of whence we come and whither go.

Achilles and Death
(Achilles speaks to Odysseus)

Renowned Odysseus, spare your breath.
Speak not to me in praise of death.
    Put me again on earth,
And let me live, yea with élan,
The hireling slave of a landless man,
    Who suffers from a dearth
Of sustenance, and let me share
His meager bread. So I would fare.

Far rather that, than reign
As lord and king o'er all the dead,
Who've done with life, who've now been sped
Down here to Death's domain.

HORACE
(65 B.C.–8 B.C.)

Desiderata

I hate the Persian luxuries,
And linden wreathes do me displease.
Seek not the lingering rose to seize,
      For no such cares be mine.
Parure the myrtle doesn't deserve;
Plain myrtle's fine for you who serve,
And too for me, who drink with verve
      Beneath the thick-grown vine.

Carpe Diem!

Seek not—'tis wrong to know, Leuconöe,
What end the gods have set for you and me.
Try not the numbers used in Babylon.
Far better, maid, to set your heart upon
Whate'er may happen, whether Zeus has massed
More years for us, or makes this one our last,
Its winter wearing down now steadily
Opposing rocks of the Etruscan Sea.
Come drink your wine; cut short long hope; be wise!
Our life span's brief. Nay, while we talk, time flies.
      Now seize the passing day;
      Let tomorrow come what may.

Glycera Calls to Venus

O Venus, reigning queen
Of Cnidus and Paphos too,
Leave Cyprus' fair scene,
For Glycera calls to you.
Come to her lovely shrine,
Where incense fills the air.
And let your son divine
Accompany you there.
And let the Nymphs and Graces,
With flowing robes, now hie
To follow in your traces.
Let Mercury draw nigh,
And Youth, whom your caress
Endows with comeliness.

To Chloe

You flee me, Chloe, like a fawn,
On pathless mountains all forlorn,
And searching for her mother now,
In silly dread of every bough
And every gentle little breeze.
She trembles so in heart and knees.
She shudders in the springtime, when
The leaves sway in the wind. Again,
She quivers, if green lizards stir,
And move the bramble next to her.
But I pursue you now, dear child,
Not like a tiger or a wild
Getúlian lion, whose wicked shim
It is, to tear you limb from limb.
    Cease trailing Mama with élan;
    It's time for you to get a MAN!

LUCILIUS
(160 B.C.–103/2 B.C.)

"Asclépiádes, the miser"

Asclépiádes, the miser
Once saw a little mouse,
And said—Dear mouse, pray tell me
What are you doing in my house?
The mouse said, smiling sweetly,—
My friend, do not be floored,
And put away your fears now.
I seek just room, NOT board!

MAECENAS
(70 B.C.–8 B.C.)

O, Stop Your Whining!

Have a pain in your hand,
In your hip; have the gout.
Have a hump on your back;
Let your loose teeth fall out.
You're living, so WHAT
ARE YOU BITCHING ABOUT?

MARTIAL
(c. 38–41 A.D.–c. 102–104 A.D.)

Change of Business

Diaulus was a doctor,
But he has turned mortician.
He now takes care of errors
He made, when a physician.

Wigs and Women

Fabúlla, Paula swears
The head of hair she wears
    Is truly all her own.
    Let well enough alone.
I do not think she errs;
She bought it. It is hers!

Promises, Promises

You promise me an awful lot,
   When you drink the night away.
The morning after, all's forgot.
   Pollio, drink by day.

You're Not on My Wave-Length

I do not like you, Mr. S;
The reason why I cannot guess.
But this I know, this I confess:—
I do not like you, Mr. S.

Wines and Widowers

The richest wines you always serve, when dining.
   They're not the greatest, Paulus, all are thinking.
Three times you widowed were, by just such wining.
   Of course, I don't believe it,—but I'm not drinking!

NICARCHUS
(fl. 1st century, A.D.)

The Great Doctor

The doctor, Marcus, laid his hand
On the statue of Zeus, they say;
And though he is Zeus, and made of stone,
He is to be buried today.

PENTADIUS
(late 2nd century, A.D.)

Entrust Your Ship to the Winds

Entrust your ship to the winds; do not dare
Entrust your heart to a maiden fair.
Safer by far are the winds of the sea
Than a woman's faith will ever be.
No woman is true. But if you should find
Such a one, by chance, bear this in mind:—
By some strange fate not understood,
An evil thing has been changed to good.

CAIUS PETRONIUS
(27 A.D.–66 A.D.)

De Gustibus

To each his heart's desire;
There are no bournes.
Some roses may acquire,
Others, thorns.

PLATO
(428/427 B.C.–348/347 B.C.)

We Are All Awaited

Of a shipwrecked man I am the tomb
A farmer's tomb is opposite me
Death lies in wait, I must assume
For all alike, on land and sea.

PLAUTUS
(254 B.C.–184 B.C.)

Epitaph

He died and comedy wept full sore;
The stage was dark, and laughter
And jokes and jests and rimes galore
All wailed together thereafter.

PUBLILIUS SYRUS
(1st century, B.C.)

Business and Luck

If you trust to luck
For your business to proceed,
Then you have before you
A pretty bad business indeed!

Some Thoughts on Delay

Although delay
You may despise,
Sometimes it may
Turn out to be wise!

SAPPHO
(c. 612 B.C.)

Dawn

In golden sandals,
Dawn, like a thief,
Has fallen upon me.

Question

Virginity, Virginity,
This I would know:
Now that you leave me,
Where do you go?
  I am gone;
  And this you may learn—
  I never come back to you,
  Never return.

The Death of Timas

This is the dust of Timas,
Who, dying still unwed,
Was led
Down to the darkened chamber
Of Persephone,
To be

Received. And when she died,
The fair
Young maidens, in despair,
With newly sharpened knives,
Sheared off their lovely hair.

The Sky

Indeed, I could not hope, think I,
With my two arms, to touch the sky.

Flower Power

Dika, find
Some shoots of dill, and wind
Them in a garland gracefully;
Then bind
Them in your lovely hair.
  The Graces kind
  Do love the girl
  Whose hair is entwined
  With flowers.

  But the girl who is
  Ungarlanded,
  They are inclined
  To spurn.

SENECA
(3 B.C.–65 A.D.)

Voracious Time

Voracious Time devours all things,
Seizes them all within her reign,
Moves everything from its primal place.
Nought is allowed for long to remain.

SIMONIDES
(556 B.C.–468 B.C.)

Timócreon's Epitaph

His eating, drinking, slandering
    Past,
Here lies Timócreon
    At last.

Theódorus Rejoices

Theódorus rejoices,
Now that I am dead.
Another will rejoice,
When HE to Death is led.
    We are all owed
    To Death's abode.

THEOGNIS
(6th century, B.C.E.)

Rejoice, My Heart

Rejoice, my heart, rejoice with me;
    For other men
    Will come again,
When I, in death, dark earth shall be.

Over the Winebowl

Over the winebowl many
    friends are true;
In grievous matters, though,
    They're rather few.

TIBULLUS
(55 B.C.–19 B.C.)

Rumor

Rumor has it that
    My lady oft deceives me.
O, would that now my ears
    Were deaf to this. It grieves me
When whisp'rings such as this
    Are noised. O, Rumor shrill,
Why is it that you rack
    And torture me? Be still!

ZENODOTUS
(fl. 280 B.C.)

On a Statue of Cupid (Love)

Who sculpted Love and placed him here
Beside this pool.
Thus thinking fire with water to quench?
He is a fool.

~

Medieval

~

ANONYMOUS LYRICS

On Marriage

They say a man
Who takes a wife
(They all concur)
Will lead a life
That's tempest-tossed
Without much bliss.
And then they marry
Knowing this!

Small Things

Small things do not revile at all,
For they possess
A pleasantness
And Cypris' son was also small.

The Rose

For such a brief time blooms the rose,
And when its season swiftly goes,
You'll seek it, if you so desire,
And find no rose, but just a brier.

Homer

The tale of a city aflame
O, Homer, you did narrate.
And the unsacked cities then came
Thereby, to envy her fate.

Youth and Age

For youth and dread old age
I mourn.
When one draws near, the other
Is gone.

I Shall Not Care

When I am dead
Let earth with fire be burned
It matters not
I shall be unconcerned.

Shipwrecked

If you save those at sea,
Dear Cypris, lend a hand
To one in need of thee,
Dying shipwrecked here on land.

Medieval Song

My love in her attire doth show her wit.
It doth so well become her:
For every season she hath dressings fit,
    For winter, spring and summer.
    No beauty she doth miss,
    When all her robes are on.
    But Beauty's self she is,
    When all her robes are gone.

ANONYMOUS
(Irish, ca. 7th century)

The Scribe: "A Hedge of Trees"

A hedge of trees surrounds me,
A blackbird's lay sings to me;
Above my lined booklet
The trilling birds chant to me.

In a grey mantle from the top of bushes
The cuckoo sings:
Verily—may the Lord shield me!—
Well do I write under the greenwood.

—*Translated from the Irish by Kuno Meyer*

ANONYMOUS
(English, 13th century)

Cuckoo Song ("Sumer is icumen in")

Sumer is ycomen in,
Loude sing cuckou!
Groweth seed and bloweth meed,
And springth the wode now.
Sing, cuckou!

Ewe bleteth after lamb,
Loweth after calve cow,
Bulloc sterteth, bucke verteth,
Merye sing cuckou!
Cuckou, cuckou,
Wel singest thou cuckou:
Ne swik thou never now!

ARCHIAS
(120 B.C.–61 B.C.)

Take Aim!

Get ready, Cypris, with your bow;
But find another mark, please do.
I've no place left at all, you know,
For another little wound from you!

BOËTHIUS
(480 A.D.–524 A.D.)

On Pleasure

With all of pleasure
   Is it thus:
With goads she ever
   Driveth us,
Who taste her joys.
   Then like unto
The flitting bee,
   Who pours forth brew
Of honey sweet,
   She doth depart
On wings of flight,
   While we do smart
From her biting sting
   Within our heart.

On Wealth

Though the rich man ever dig indeed
From his mine of gold, for wealth galore,
(That ne'er will satisfy his need);
Though precious pearls from the Red Sea's shore
Adorn his neck, and though he plow
Rich fields, with a hundred oxen, still
Dread biting care will not allow
Calm peace of mind at all, until
He seek Death's realm, there but to find
That fickle Wealth remains behind.

CAPITO
(fl. 600 B.C.)

Beauty and Charm

Beauty sans charm may captivate
But does not last, for look—
It's merely like the fishing bait
That floats without the hook.

DEMODOCUS

There's Always the Unexpected!

An evil viper once
A Cappadócian bit,
But tasting poisoned blood,
The VIPER died of it!

DION OF TARSUS

Dion Writes His Epitaph

Dion of Tarsus lies here dead,
Sixty years old, and never wed.
Would this were true
Of my father too.

DIONYSIUS THE SOPHIST

Rose Girl

Rose girl, you with the rosy charm,
Pray tell,
Is it your roses, yourself, or both
That you sell?

ERATÓSTHENES
(276 B.C.–195 B.C.)

Daphnis to Pan

Daphnis, lover of women
Dedicates with elan
This club and skin and pipe
To his beloved Pan.
O Pan, these gifts of Daphnis
I pray you to receive;
Like him, you welcome music;
Like him, in love, you grieve.

HITOMARO
(662 A.D.–710 A.D.)

Prayer for the Men After Me

May the men who are born
From my time onward
Never, never meet
With a path of love-making
Such as mine has been.

LADY HORIKAWA
(13th century)

True Love

How can one e'er be sure
If true love will endure?
My thoughts this morning are
As tangled as my hair.

JULIANUS, PREFECT OF EGYPT
(6th century)

Love Among the Roses

While weaving a garland
One fine day,
I found that midst
The roses lay
The god of Love.
I picked him up,
And dipped him in
The wine-filled cup.
I took and drank him;
Now he clings
Inside me, tickling
With his wings.

Advice to the Thieves

Seek other, more gainful houses, thieves,
For Poverty always guards these eaves.

LI PO
(701 A.D.–762 A.D.)

The Girl of Yueh

She is gathering lotus seeds in the river of Yueh.
While singing, she sees a stranger, and turns around.
Then she smiles and hides among the lotus leaves,
Pretending to be overcome by shyness.

A Meeting

They met in the red dust.
He raised his yellow-gold crop in salutation.
"There are ten thousand houses among the drooping willows.
O Lady, where are you living?"

In the Mountains on a Summer Day

Gently I stir a white feather fan,
With open shirt, sitting in a green wood.
I take off my cap and hang it on a jutting stone.
A wind from the pine tree trickles on my bare head.

MACEDONIUS THE CONSUL
(500 A.D.–560 A.D.)

To Eros

Cease, Love, to throw your dart
At my liver and my heart
    But if you're bent
    On this intent,
Aim at another part!

Memory and Oblivion

To Memory and Oblivion
All hail, I hereby say—
Oblivion, when times are sad,
And Memory, when they're gay.

MELEAGER
(1st century, B.C.)

Heliodóra's Garland

The flowers are fading that entwine
My Heliodóra's brow.
And Heliodóra doth outshine
The garland's flowers now.

To Timarion

Your kiss is mistletoe.
Your eyes are fire bright.
One look, Timarion,
From you, and I ignite.
One touch from you, and I
Am bound and fettered tight.

PALLADAS
(4th century, A.D.)

The Double-Minded

I hate the double-minded who mislead.
They may be friends in word, but not in deed.

Life Is a Stage

All life is a stage and a play
Either learn to sport and jest,
Putting seriousness away
Or live, by griefs oppressed.

PETRARCH
(1304–1374)

Sonnet 1

O ye who in these scattered rhymes may hear
The echoes of the sighs that fed my heart
In errant youth, for I was then, in part
Another man from what I now appear,
If you have learned by proof how Love can sear,
Then for these varied verses where I chart
Its vain and empty hope and vainer smart
Pardon I may beseech, nay, Pity's tear.
For now I see how once my story spread
And I became a wonder to mankind
So in my heart I feel ashamed—alas,
That nought but shame my vanities have bred,
And penance, and the knowledge of clear mind
That earthly joys are dreams that swiftly pass.

Sonnet 104

I find no peace and bear no arms for war,
I fear, I hope; I burn yet shake with chill;
I fly the Heavens, huddle to earth's floor,
Embrace the world yet all I grasp is nil.
Love opens not nor shuts my prison's door
Nor claims me his nor leaves me to my will;
He slays me not yet holds me evermore,
Would have me lifeless yet bound to my ill.

Eyeless I see and tongueless I protest,
And long to perish while I succor seek;
Myself I hate and would another woo.
I feed on grief, I laugh with sob-racked breast
And death and life alike to me are bleak:
My Lady, thus I am because of you.

SADI
(1184–1283/1291)

Hyacinths

If of thy mortal goods thou art bereft,
And from thy slender store two loaves to thee are left,
Sell one, and with the dole,
Buy hyacinths to feed thy soul.

STRABO
(64/63 B.C.–24 A.D.)

Kiss Me, Sweet!

If I do wrong, by kissing you
And you think this a sin to do,
Then YOU kiss ME, and you will vent
On ME the same, as punishment!

Share and Share Alike

If Beauty ages
Then, my heart
Give me some
Ere it depart.

But if it stays
Then why disdain
To give me what
Will e'er remain?

SU T'UNG-PO
(1037–1101)

On the Birth of His Son

Families, when a child is born,
Want it to be intelligent.
I, through intelligence.
Having wrecked my whole life,
Only hope the baby will prove
Ignorant and stupid.
Then he will crown a tranquil life
By becoming a Cabinet Minister.

FRANÇOIS VILLON
(1431–1463)

Death Seizes All

I know the rich and poor, I say,
The wise and foolish, priest and lay,
The nobles, villains, kind and mean,
The little and big, the pure and obscene,
The ladies with furs and many a jewel—
Death seizes them all within her rule.

Rondeau

Death, against thee I inveigh.
Thou hast my mistress taken away.
Nor art thou satisfied until
Thou hold me too, against my will,
All lacking in strength and force for strife;
How did she harm thee then in life,
           Death?
One heart was ours, though we were twain.
If she be dead, then would I fain
Die too, or else must I exist
Sans life, like shadows in a mist,
           Death.

Ballade

Herewith ends the last testament
Of the poor François Villon;
Pray come to his interment,
When you hear the carillon.
Come dressed in vermillion red,
For he was love's martyr at heart.
Swore he this on his own deathbed,
When he wished from this life to depart.

YAKAMOCHI
(718? A.D.–785 A.D.)

By Way of Pretext

By way of pretext
I said, "I will go
And look at
The condition of the bamboo fence."
But it was really to see you!

Early Modern

≈

ANONYMOUS

The Calvinist

Eat it up; wear it out.
Make it do; do without.

ANONYMOUS
(French, 18th century)

An Observation

The world is a strange affair.
So said Jean-Baptiste Molière.
So sayeth I; but "Que faire?"

WILLIAM BLAKE
(1757–1827)

The Fly

Little Fly,
Thy summer's play
My thoughtless hand
Has brushed away.

Am not I
A fly like thee?
Or art not thou
A man like me?

For I dance
And drink, and sing,
Till some blind hand
Shall brush my wing.

If thought is life
And strength and breath
And the want
Of thought is death;

Then am I
A happy fly,
If I live,
Or if I die.

ROBERT BURNS
(1759–1796)

John Anderson My Jo

John Anderson my jo, John
  When we were first acquent,
Your locks were like the raven,
  Your bonnie brow was brent.

But now your brow is beld, John,
    Your locks are like the snaw;
But blessings on your frosty pow,
    John Anderson my jo.
John Anderson, my jo, John,
    We clamb the hill thegither;
And many a canty day, John,
    We've had wi' ane anither.
Now we maun totter down, John,
    And hand in hand we'll go,
And sleep thegither at the foot,
    John Anderson my jo.

THOMAS CAMPION
(1567–1620)

"When to her lute Corinna sings"

When to her lute Corinna sings,
Her voice revives the leaden strings,
And doth in highest notes appear
As any challenged echo clear;
But when she doth of mourning speak,
Ev'n with her sighs the strings do break.
And as her lute doth live or die,
Let by her passion, so must I:
For when of pleasure she doth sing,
My thoughts enjoy a sudden spring,
But if she doth of sorrow speak,
Ev'n from my heart the strings do break.

ABRAHAM COWLEY
(1618–1667)

The Epicure

Fill the bowl with rosy wine,
Around our temples roses twine,
And let us cheerfully awhile
Like the wine and roses smile.
Crowned with roses, we contemn
Gyges' wealthy diadem.
Today is ours; what do we fear?
Today is ours; we have it here.
Let's treat it kindly, that it may
Wish, at least, with us to stay.
Let's banish business, banish sorrow;
To the gods belongs tomorrow.

RICHARD CRASHAW
(c. 1613–1649)

The World's Light Shines

The world's light shines, shine as it will,
The world will love its darkness still.
I doubt though, when the world's in hell,
It will not love its darkness half so well.

PHILIPPE DESPORTES
(1546–1606)

Icarus

Here Icarus died, young lad unbowed,
Who flew up to Heaven, with courage avowed.
Here lies the body—no plumage at all;
Let other brave souls all envy his fall.
O beautiful task of a high-flowing heart,
That gives rich reward, all sadness apart.
O fortunate sorrow, with this to be said—
It renders the vanquished, the victor instead.
A path so untried did NOT shock his youth.
'Twas power that failed him, not valor, in truth.
He was burned by the stars for what he was doing.
He perished, a glorious venture pursuing.
The sky was his dream; the sea was his doom;
Where is nobler theme or richer tomb?

JOHN DONNE
(1572–1631)

Death, Be Not Proud

Death, be not proud, though some have callèd thee
Mighty and dreadful, for thou art not so;
For those whom thou think'st thou dost overthrow
Die not, poor death, nor yet canst thou kill me.
From rest and sleep, which but thy pictures be,
Much pleasure; then from thee much more must flow,
And soonest our best men with thee do go,
Rest of their bones, and soul's delivery.
Thou'rt slave to fate, chance, kings, and desperate men,
And dost with poison, war, and sickness dwell;
And poppy or charms can make us sleep as well
And better then thy stroke; why swell'st thou then?
One short sleep past, we wake eternally,
And death shall be no more; Death, thou shalt die.

BENJAMIN FRANKLIN
(1706–1790)
(From Poor Richard's Almanac)

A Light Purse

A light purse
Is a heavy curse.

Great Spenders

Great spenders
Are bad lenders.

He that goes a-borrowing

He that goes a-borrowing
Goes a-sorrowing.

JOHN GAY
(1685–1732)

His Epitaph

Life is a jest
And all things show it;
I thought so once,
But now I know it.

JOHANN WOLFGANG VON GOETHE
(1749–1832)

Nightsong

Now is there silence on the hill;
In all the treetops the silence is deep.
The birds in the wood are hushed and still.
Ah wait, for soon thou too shalt sleep.

BARNABE GOOGE
(1540–1594)

A Posy

Two lines shall tell the grief that I by love sustain—
I burn, I flame, I freeze, of hell I feel the pain.

JOHN HARINGTON
(1561–1612)

Comparison of the Sonnet and the Epigram

Once, by mishap, two poets fell a-squaring,
The sonnet, and our epigram comparing;
And Faustus, having long demur'd upon it,
Yet, at the last, gave sentence for the sonnet.
Now, for such censure, this his chief defence is,
Their sugared taste best likes his lickerish senses.
     Well, though I grant sugar may please the taste,
     Yet let my verse have salt to make it last.

GEORGE HERBERT
(1593–1633)

The Quiddity

My God, a verse is not a crown,
No point of honour, or gay suit,
No hawk, or banquet, or renown,
Nor a good sword, nor yet a lute.

It cannot vault, or dance, or play;
It never was in France or Spain;
Nor can it entertain the day
With a great stable or domain.

It is no office, art, or news;
Nor the Exchange, or busy Hall:
But it is that which, while I use,
I am with Thee: and *Most take all*.

ROBERT HERRICK
(1591–1674)

The Present Time Best Pleaseth

Praise they that will Times past; I joy to see
My selfe now live; this age best pleaseth me.

Upon Julia's Voice

So smooth, so sweet, so silv'ry is thy voice,
As, could they hear, the Damn'd would make no noise,
But listen to thee (walking in thy chamber)
Melting melodious words, to lutes of amber.

How Lilies Came White

White though ye be; yet, Lilies, know,
From the first ye were not so;
   But I'll tell ye
   What befell ye;
Cupid and his Mother lay
In a cloud; while both did play,
He with his pretty finger prest
The ruby niplet of her breast;
Out of the which, the cream of light,
   Like to a dew,
   Fell down on you,
   And made ye white.

A Sweet Disorder

A sweet disorder in the dress
Kindles in clothes a wantonness;
A lawn about the shoulders thrown
Into a fine distraction—
An erring lace, which here and there
Enthrals the crimson stomacher—
A cuff neglectful, and thereby
Ribbands to flow confusedly—
A winning wave, deserving note,
In the tempestuous petticoat—
A careless shoe-string, in whose tie
I see a wild civility—
Do more bewitch me than when art
Is too precise in every part.

BEN JONSON
(1572–1637)

The Noble Nature

It is not growing like a tree
  In bulk, doth make Man better be;
Or standing long an oak, three hundred year,
To fall a log at last, dry, bald and sere;
  A lily of a day
  Is fairer far in May.
Although it fall and die that night—
It was the plant and flower of Light.
In small proportions we just beauties see;
And in short measures life may perfect be.

Epitaph on the Countess Dowager of Pembroke

Underneath the sable hearse
Lies the subject of all verse,
Sidney's sister, Pembroke's mother.
Death, ere thou has slain another,
Learned and fair and good is she,
Time shall throw a dart at thee.

On My First Daughter

Here lies, to each her parents' ruth,
Mary, the daughter of her youth;
Yet all heaven's gifts being heaven's due,
It makes the father less to rue.
At six months' end she parted hence
With safety of her innocence;
Whose soul heaven's queen, whose name she bears,
In comfort of her mother's tears,

Hath placed amongst her virgin-train:
Where, while that severed doth remain,
This grave partakes the fleshly birth;
Which cover lightly, gentle earth!

Why I Write Not of Love

Some act of Love's bound to rehearse,
I thought to bind him in my verse:
Which when he felt, Away, quoth he,
Can poets hope to fetter me?
It is enough, they once did get
Mars and my mother, in their net:
I wear not these my wings in vain.
With which he fled me; and again,
Into my rhymes could ne'er be got
By any art: then wonder not,
That since, my numbers are so cold,
When Love is fled, and I grow cold.

JOHN LYLY
(1553–1606)

Cupid and Campáspe

Cupid and my Campáspe play'd
At cards for kisses; Cupid paid;
He stakes his quiver, bow, and arrows,
His mother's doves, and team of sparrows;
Loses them too; then down he throws
The coral of his lip, the rose
Growing one's cheek (but none knows how);
With these the crystal of his brow,
And then the dimple on his chin;
All these did my Campáspe win;

At last he set her both his eyes—
She won, and Cupid blind did rise.
　O Love! has she done this to thee?
　What shall, alas, become of me?

CHRISTOPHER MARLOWE
(1564–1593)

Helen
From Dr. Faustus

Was this the face that launched a thousand ships
And burnt the topless towers of Ilium?
Sweet Helen, make me immortal with a kiss.
Her lips suck forth my soul; see where it flies.
Come, Helen, come, give me my soul again.
Here will I dwell, for Heaven be in these lips,
And all is dross that is not Helena.

JOHN MILTON
(1608–1674)

Song On May Morning

Now the bright morning star, day's harbinger,
Comes dancing from the East, and leads with her
The Flowry May, who from her green lap throws
The yellow Cowslip, and the pale Primrose.
　　Hail Bounteous May that dost inspire
　　Mirth and youth, and warm desire;
　　Woods and groves are of thy dressing,
　　Hill and dale doth boast thy blessing.
Thus we salute thee with our early song,
And welcome thee, and wish thee long.

WILLIAM OLDYS
(1696–1761)

On a Fly Drinking Out of His Cup

Busy, curious, thirsty fly!
Drink with me and drink as I;
Freely welcome to my cup,
Couldst thou sip and sip it up.
Make the most of life you may,
Life is short and wears away.

Both alike are mine and thine,
Hastening quick to their decline.
Thine's a summer, mine's no more,
Though repeated to three score.
Three score summers, when they're gone,
Will appear as short as one!

THOMAS PARNELL
(1679–1718)

Song

When thy beauty appears,
    In its graces and airs,
All bright as an angel new dropped from the sky;
    At distance I gaze, and am awed by my fears
    So strangely you dazzle my eye!

But when without art,
    Your kind thoughts you impart,
When your love runs in blushes through every vein;
    When it darts from your eyes, when it pants in your heart,
    Then I know you're a woman again.

"There's a passion and pride
    In our sex," she replied,
"And thus (might I gratify both) I would do;
    Still an angel appear to each lover beside,
    But still be a woman to you."

WALTER RALEIGH
(1552–1618)

Epitaph

Even such is time, which takes in trust
Our youth, our joys, and all we have,
And pays us but with age and dust,
Who in the dark and silent grave
When we have wandered all our ways
Shuts up the story of our days,
And from which earth, and grave, and dust
The Lord will raise me up, I trust.

MATHURIN RÉGNIER
(1573–1613)

His Epitaph

I've lived my life sans stress or care,
Wandering freely here and there,
      For I to Nature's laws defer.
And so I am astonished now,
That Death has deigned to think somehow
      Of me, who never thought of her.

PIERRE DE RONSARD
(1524–1585)

To His Soul

My little soul, my very own,
My sweet and gentle friend,
The well loved guest of my body, now
To the lower world you descend,

All weak and pale and thin, alone
In Death's vast cold domain;
Yet simple, sans remorse for shame,
For rancor or ill gain.

And spurning favors, treasured wealth
That other men do need.
You pass me by; I say to you—
Go where your fortunes lead.
Now my repose is deep.
Disturb it not; I sleep.

SIR WALTER SCOTT
(1771–1832)

Proud Maisie

Proud Maisie is in the wood,
    Walking so early;
Sweet Robin sits on the bush
    Singing so rarely.

"Tell me, thou bonny bird,
    When shall I marry me?"
"When six braw gentlemen
    Kirkward shall carry ye."

"Who makes the bridal bed,
    Birdie, say truly?"
The gray-headed sexton
    That delves the grave duly.

"The glowworm o'er grave and stone
    Shall light thee steady;
The owl from the steeple sing,
    'Welcome, proud lady.'"

My Native Land

Breathes there the man, with soul so dead,
Who never to himself hath said,
This is my own, my native land!
Whose heart hath ne'er within him burned,
As home his footsteps he hath turned,
From wandering on a foreign strand!
If such there breathe, go, mark him well;
For him no Minstrel raptures swell;
High though his titles, proud his name,
Boundless his wealth as wish can claim;
Despite those titles, power, and pelf,
The wretch, concentred all in self,
Living, shall forfeit fair renown,
And, doubly dying, shall go down
To the vile dust, from whence he sprung,
Unwept, unhonored, and unsung.

SIR CHARLES SEDLEY
(1639–1701)

Song

Phillis is my only joy,
    Faithless as the winds or seas;
Sometimes coming, sometimes coy.
    Yet she never fails to please;
        If with a frown
        I am cast down,
        Phillis smiling,
        And beguiling,
Makes me happier than before.
Though, alas, too late I find,
    Nothing can her fancy fix;
Yet the moment she is kind,
    I forgive her all her tricks;
        Which, though I see,

I can't get free;
She deceiving,
I believing;
What can lovers wish for more?

WILLIAM SHAKESPEARE
(1564–1616)

Sonnet CLIV

The little Love-god lying once asleep
Laid by his side his heart-inflaming brand,
Whilst many nymphs that vow'd chaste life to keep
Came tripping by; but in her maiden hand
The fairest votary took up that fire
Which many legions of true hearts had warm'd;
And so the general of hot desire
Was sleeping by a virgin hand disarm'd.
This brand she quenched in a cool well by,
Which from Love's fire took heat perpetual,
Growing a bath and healthful remedy
For men diseas'd; but I, my mistress' thrall,
    Came there for cure, and this by that I prove,
    Love's fire heats water, water cools not love.

Sonnet LV

Not marble nor the gilded monuments
Of princes shall outlive this powerful rhyme;
But you shall shine more bright in these contents
Than unswept stone, besmear'd with sluttish time.
When wasteful war shall statues overturn,
And broils root out the work of masonry,
Nor Mars his sword nor war's quick fire shall burn
The living record of your memory.
'Gainst death and all-oblivious enmity
Shall you pace forth; your praise shall still find room,

Even in the eyes of all posterity
That wear this world out to the ending doom.
  So, till the judgment that yourself arise,
  You live in this, and dwell in lovers' eyes.

Ariel's Warning
From The Tempest

While you here do snoring lie,
Open-eyed conspiracy
  His time doth take:
If of life you keep a care,
Shake off slumber, and beware:
  Awake! Awake!

Full Fathom Five
From The Tempest

Full fathom five thy father lies;
  Of his bones are coral made:
Those are pearls that were his eyes:
  Nothing of him that doth fade,
But doth suffer a sea-change
Into something rich and strange.
Sea-nymphs hourly ring his knell:
  Ding-dong.
Hark! now I hear them,—
Ding-dong, bell.

JAMES SHIRLEY
(1596–1666)

On Her Dancing

I stood and saw my mistress dance,
Silent, and with so fixed an eye,
Some might suppose me in a trance.
But being asked why,
By one who knew I was in love,
I could not but impart
My wonder, to behold her move
So nimbly with a marble heart.

Good-night

Bid me no more good-night; because
　'Tis dark, must I away?
Love doth acknowledge no such laws,
　And Love 'tis I obey,
Which, blind, doth all your light despise,
　　And hath no need of eyes
　　　When day is fled;
Besides, the sun, which you
Complain is gone, 'tis true,
　　　Is gone to bed:
　　　Oh, let us do so too.

PHILIP SIDNEY
(1554–1586)

My True-Love Hath My Heart

My true-love hath my heart and I have his,
By just exchange, one for another given;
I hold his dear, and mine he cannot miss.
There never was a better bargain driven.

My true-love hath my heart, and I have his.
His heart in him his thought and senses guides.
He loves my heart, for once it was his own,
I cherish his, because in me it bides.
My true-love hath my heart and I have his.

EDMUND SPENSER
(c. 1552–1599)

One Day I Wrote Her Name

One day I wrote her name upon the strand,
But came the waves and washèd it away.
Again I wrote it with a second hand,
But came the tide and made my pains his prey.
"Vain man" said she, "that dost in vain essay
A mortal thing so to immortalize;
For I myself shall, like to this, decay,
And eke my name be wiped out likewise."
"Not so" quoth I, "let baser thing devise
To die in dust, but you shall live by fame;
My verse your virtues rare shall eternize.
And in the heavens write your glorious name;
Where, whenas Death shall all the world subdue,
Our love shall live, and later life renew."

SIR JOHN SUCKLING
(1609–1642)

Song

Why so pale and wan, fond lover?
Prithee, why so pale?—
Will, when looking well can't move her,
Looking ail prevail?
Prithee, why so pale?

Why so dull and mute, young sinner?
Prithee, why so mute?—
Will, when speaking well can't win her,
Saying nothing do't?
Prithee, why so mute?

Quit, quit, for shame! this will not move,
This cannot take her—
If of herself she will not love,
Nothing can make her:
The Devil take her!

JONATHAN SWIFT
(1667–1745)

On Stella's Birthday

Stella this day is thirty-four,
(We won't dispute a year or more:)
However, Stella, be not troubled,
Although thy size and years are doubled
Since first I saw thee at sixteen,
The brightest virgin on the green;
So little is thy form declined,
Made up so largely in thy mind.
      O, would it please the gods to split
Thy beauty, size, and years, and wit,
No age could furnish out a pair
Of nymphs so graceful, wise, and fair;
With half the lustre of your eyes,
With half your wit, your years and size.
And then, before it grew too late,
How should I beg of gentle Fate,
(That either nymph might have her swain)
To split my worship too in twain.

VOLTAIRE
(1694–1778)

Epigrams
Inscription for a Statue of Cupid

Whoever you are, your master is here.
He is, he was, or should be, 'tis clear.

Jeremiah

Do you know why Jeremiah's tears
Could never be abated?
'Tis that, as prophet, he foresaw
That by Lefranc he'd be translated.

Jean Fréron

The other day, in a valley, alas,
A serpent bit Fréron, 'tis said.
And what do you think then came to pass?
It was the SERPENT that dropped dead.

An Epitaph

Here lies one whose loss supreme
Was to live FOR HIMSELF; that was his theme.
But passer-by, beware of him;
Do not attempt to follow his whim;
For, on your tomb, the world will scrawl—
Here he lies, who never should have lived at all!

EDMUND WALLER
(1606–1687)

Song

Stay, Phoebus, stay!
The world to which you fly so fast
Conveying day
From us to them, can pay your haste
With no such object, nor salute your rise
With no such wonder as DeMornay's eyes.

Well does this prove
The error of those antique books,
Which made you move
About the world; her charming looks
Would fix your beams, and make it every day,
Did not the rolling earth snatch her away.

On a Girdle

That which her slender waist confin'd,
Shall now my joyful temples bind;
No monarch but would give his crown,
His arms might do what this has done.

It was my heaven's extremest sphere,
The pale which held that lovely deer,
My joy, my grief, my hope, my love,
Did all within this circle move.

A narrow compass, and yet there
Dwelt all that's good, and all that's fair;
Give me but what this ribbon bound,
Take all the rest the sun goes round.

SIR HENRY WOTTON
(1568–1639)

Upon the Death of Sir Albert Morton's Wife

He first deceased, she for a little tried
To live without him, liked it not, and died.

~

Nineteenth Century

~

THOMAS BAILEY ALDRICH
(1836–1907)

"I would be the Lyric"

I would be the Lyric
Ever on the lip,
Rather than the Epic
Memory lets slip.
I would be the diamond
At my lady's ear,
Rather than the June-rose
Worn but once a year.

Realism

Romance beside his unstrung lute
Lies stricken mute.
The old-time fire, the antique grace,
You will not find them anywhere.
To-day we breathe a commonplace,
Polemic, scientific air:
We strip Illusion of her veil;

We vivisect the nightingale
To probe the secret of his note.
The Muse in alien ways remote
Goes wandering.

"Pillared arch and sculptured tower"

Pillared arch and sculptured tower
Of Ilium have had their hour;
The dust of many a king is blown
On the winds from zone to zone;
Many a warrior sleeps unknown.
Time and Death hold each in thrall,
Yet is Love the lord of all;
Still does Helen's beauty stir
Because a poet sang of her.

WILLIAM ALLINGHAM
(1824–1889)

Four Ducks on a Pond

Four ducks on a pond,
A grass-bank beyond,
A blue sky of spring,
White clouds on the wing;
What a little thing
To remember for years—
To remember with tears!

MATTHEW ARNOLD
(1822–1888)

Requiescat

Strew on her roses, roses,
    And never a spray of yew!
In quiet she reposes;
    Ah, would that I did too!

Her mirth the world required;
    She bathed it in smiles of glee.
But her heart was tired, tired,
    And now they let her be.

Her life was turning, turning,
    In mazes of heat and sound.
But for peace her soul was yearning,
    And now peace laps her round.

Her cabin'd, ample spirit,
    It flutter'd and fail'd for breath.
To-night it doth inherit
    The vasty hall of death.

FÉLIX ARVERS
(1806–1850)

A Secret

My soul has its secret, mysterious, deep,
An eternal amour, in one moment conceived.
All hopeless it is, all silent I've been,
And she who inspired me never perceived.
Alas, I'll have passed all my life next to her,
Unnoticed, alone. I shall live on, nor dare
To ask or receive any favor or grace.
And she whom God made so gentle and fair,

Goes her way, hearing not the whispers of love.
Pious and pure, she will take in her hand
These verses, all filled with her, read them and say,
"But who is this woman?" and will not understand.

CHARLES BAUDELAIRE
(1821–1867)

The Voyage

Oh Death, old captain, raise anchor; 'tis dark.
This life here but bores us. Oh Death, now embark!
Black as ink are the sky and the sea below,
But the rays of light fill our hearts; this you know.

Oh pour forth your poison, to soothe! We desire
(So much is our brain inflamed by this fire)
To plunge to the depths of the gulf, hear the knell.
For what does it matter—Heaven or hell—
If only the vast unknown we may view,
There to find something new, something NEW!

GEORGE HENRY BOKER
(1823–1890)

Sonnet

If Grecian Helen pleaded with the tongue
The Chian lent her—sweetest tongue of earth!
If Agamemnon's child forgot her birth,
And at my knee in panting beauty clung;
If fiery Cleopatra sued and hung
Fast to my restless hand in prurient mirth;
If chaste Lucretia wrecked her ancient worth;
And Rosamond's hair about my face were flung;
If all the fairest creatures that have worn
The poets' wreaths, the crowns of chivalry,

Were singly or in concourse offered me;
I would reject, in haste and simple scorn
The night-born stars, whose rise foreran thy morn,
Yea, from their homage turn to worship thee.

EMILY BRONTË
(1818–1848)

"The night is darkening round me"

The night is darkening round me,
The wild winds coldly blow;
But a tyrant spell has bound me,
And I cannot, cannot go.

The giant trees are bending
Their bare boughs weighed with snow;
The storm is fast descending,
And yet I cannot go.

Clouds beyond clouds above me,
Wastes beyond wastes below;
But nothing drear can move me;
I will not, cannot go.

ELIZABETH BARRETT BROWNING
(1806–1861)

Sonnet VI

Go from me. Yet I feel that I shall stand
Henceforth in thy shadow. Nevermore
Alone upon the threshold of my door
Of individual life, I shall command
The uses of my soul, nor lift my hand
Serenely in the sunshine as before,
Without the sense of that which I forbore—
Thy touch upon the palm. The widest land

Doom takes to part us, leaves thy heart in mine
With pulses that beat double. What I do
And what I dream include thee, as the wine
Must taste of its own grapes. And when I sue
God for myself, He hears that name of thine,
And sees within my eyes the tears of two.

Sonnet XIV

If thou must love me, let it be for nought
Except for love's sake only. Do not say
"I love her for her smile—her look—her way
Of speaking gently,—for a trick of thought
That falls in well with mine, and certes brought
A sense of ease on such a day—"
For these things in themselves, Beloved, may
Be changed, or change for thee,—and love, so wrought,
May be unwrought so. Neither love me for
Thine own dear pity's wiping my cheek dry,—
A creature might forget to weep, who bore
Thy comfort long, and lose thy love thereby!
But love me for love's sake, that evermore
Thou may'st love on, through love's eternity.

ROBERT BROWNING
(1812–1889)

Speculative

Others may need new life in Heaven —
Man, Nature, Art —made new, assume!

Man with new mind old sense to leaven,
Nature —new light to clear old gloom,

Art that breaks bounds, gets soaring-room.

I shall pray: "Fugitive as precious —
Minutes which passed, —return, remain!

Let earth's old life once more enmesh us,
You with old pleasure, me —old pain,

So we but meet nor part again!"

Home Thoughts, From Abroad

Oh, to be in England
Now that April's there,
And whoever wakes in England
Sees, some morning, unaware,
That the lowest boughs and the brush-wood sheaf
Round the elm-tree bole are in tiny leaf,
While the chaffinch sings on the orchard bough
In England—now!
And after April, when May follows,
And the whitethroat builds, and all the swallows!
Hark, where my blossomed pear-tree in the hedge
Leans to the field and scatters on the clover
Blossoms and dewdrops—at the bent spray's edge—
That's the wise thrush; he sings each song twice over,
Lest you should think he never could recapture
The first fine careless rapture!
And though the fields look rough with hoary dew,
All will be gay when noontide wakes anew
The buttercups, the little children's dower
—Far brighter than this gaudy melon-flower!

GEORGE GORDON, LORD BYRON
(1788–1824)

On the Bust of Helen by Canova

In this belovèd marble view,
    Above the works and thoughts of man,
What Nature COULD, but WOULD NOT, do,
    And Beauty and Canova CAN!

Beyond imagination's power,
 Beyond the Bard's defeated art,
With immortality her dower,
 Behold the HELEN of the heart!

The Origin of Love

The "Origin of Love!"—Ah why
 That cruel question ask of me,
When thou may'st read in many an eye
 He starts to life on seeing thee?

And should'st thou seek his end to know:
 My heart forebodes, my fears foresee
He'll linger long in silent woe;
 But live—until I cease to be.

Epigram

 The world is a bundle of hay;
 Mankind are the asses who pull;
 Each tugs it a different way,—
 And the greatest of all is John Bull!

"So, we'll no more go a roving"

So, we'll no more go a roving
 So late into the night,
Though the heart be still as loving,
And the moon be still as bright.
 For the sword outwears its sheath,
And the soul wears out the breast,
And the heart must pause to breathe,
And Love itself have rest.

Though the night was made for loving,
And the day returns too soon,
Yet we'll go no more a roving
By the light of the moon.

LEWIS CARROLL
(1832–1898)

"Speak roughly to your little boy"

Speak roughly to your little boy,
    And beat him when he sneezes;
He only does it to annoy,
    Because he knows it teases!

JOHN CLARE
(1793–1864)

Stonepit

The passing traveller with wonder sees
A deep and ancient stonepit full of trees;
So deep and very deep the place has been,
The church might stand within and not be seen.
The passing stranger oft with wonder stops
And thinks he een could walk upon their tops,
And often stoops to see the busy crow,
And stands above and sees the eggs below;
And while the wild horse gives its head a toss,
The squirrel dances up and runs across.
The boy that stands and kills the black nosed bee
Dares down as soon as magpies' nests are found,
And wonders when he climbs the highest tree
To find it reaches scarce above the ground.

STEPHEN CRANE
(1871–1900)

"A Man Said to the Universe"

A man said to the universe:
"Sir I exist!"
"However," replied the universe,
"The fact has not created in me
A sense of obligation."

"Think As I Think"

"Think as I think," said a man,
"Or you are abominably wicked;
You are a toad."
And after I had thought of it,
I said, "I will then, be a toad."

"The Wayfarer"

The wayfarer,
Perceiving the pathway to truth,
Was struck with astonishment.
It was thickly grown with weeds.
"Ha," he said,
"I see that none has passed here
In a long time."
Later he saw that each weed
Was a singular knife.
"Well," he mumbled at last,
"Doubtless there are other roads."

"In Heaven"

In heaven,
Some little blades of grass
Stood before God.
"What did you do?"
Then all save one of the little blades
Began eagerly to relate
The merits of their lives.
This one stayed a small way behind,
Ashamed.
Presently, God said,
"And what did you do?"
The little blade answered, "Oh my Lord,
Memory is bitter to me,
For, if I did good deeds,
I know not of them."
Then God, in all His splendor,
Arose from His throne.
"Oh, best little blade of grass!" He said.

"Legends" (III)

A man said: "Thou tree!"
The tree answered with the same scorn: "Thou man!
Thou art greater than I only in thy possibilities."

EMILY DICKINSON
(1830–1886)

"Partake as doth the Bee"

Partake as doth the Bee,
Abstemiously.
The Rose is an Estate —
In Sicily.

"A word is dead"

A word is dead
When it is said,
Some say.

I say it just
Begins to live
That day.

"I have no life but this"

I have no Life but this—
To lead it here—
Nor any Death—but lest
Dispelled from there—

Nor tie to Earths to come—
Nor Action new—
Except through this extent—
The Realm of you—

"There is no frigate like a book"

There is no Frigate like a Book
To take us Lands away
Nor any Coursers like a Page
Of prancing Poetry—
This Traverse may the poorest take
Without oppress of Toll—
How frugal is the Chariot
That bears the Human soul.

"Not knowing when the dawn will come"

Not knowing when the Dawn will come,
I open every Door,
Or has it Feathers, like a Bird,
Or Billows, like a Shore—

"The Golden Fleece"

Finding is the first Act
The second, loss,
Third, Expedition for
The "Golden Fleece"

Fourth, no Discovery—
Fifth, no Crew—
Finally, no Golden Fleece—
Jason—sham—too.

AUSTIN DOBSON
(1840–1921)

A Kiss

Rose kissed me to-day.
Will she kiss me tomorrow?
Let it be as it may,
Rose kissed me today.
But the pleasure gives way
To a savour of sorrow;—
Rose kissed me to-day,—
Will she kiss me tomorrow?

The Wanderer

Love comes back to his vacant dwelling,—
The old, old Love that we knew of yore!
We see him stand by the open door,
With his great eyes sad, and his bosom swelling.

He makes as though in our arms repelling,
He fain would lie as he lay before;—
Love comes back to his vacant dwelling,
The old, old Love that we knew of yore!

Ah, who shall help us from over-spelling
That sweet, forgotten, forbidden lore!
E'en as we doubt in our heart once more,
With a rush of tears to our eyelids welling,
Love comes back to his vacant dwelling.

DIGBY MACKWORTH DOLBEN
(1848–1867)

Requests

I asked for Peace—
My sins arose,
And bound me close,
I could not find release.

I asked for Truth—
My doubts came in,
And with their din
They wearied all my youth.

I asked for Love—
My lovers failed,
And griefs assailed
Around, beneath, above.

I asked for Thee—
And Thou didst come
To take me home,
Within Thy Heart to be.

RALPH WALDO EMERSON
(1803–1882)

"Let me go wherever I will"

Let me go wherever I will.
I hear a sky-born music still:
It sounds from all things old,
It sounds from all things young,
From all that's fair, from all that's foul,
Peals out a cheerful song.

It is not only in the rose,
It is not only in the bird,
Not only where the rainbow glows,
Nor in the song of woman heard,
But in the darkest, meanest things
There always, always something sings.

'Tis not in the high stars alone,
Nor in the cup of budding flowers,
Nor in the redbreast's mellow tone,
Nor in the bow that smiles in showers,
But in the mud and scum of things
There always, always something sings.

THOMAS HARDY
(1840–1928)

Waiting Both

A star looks down at me,
And says: "Here I and you
Stand each in our degree:
What do you mean to do,—
  Mean to do?"

I say: "For all I know,
Wait, and let Time go by,
Till my change come."—"Just so,"
The star says: "So mean I:—
  So mean I."

Her Initials

Upon a poet's page I wrote
Of old two letters of her name;
Part seemed she of the effulgent thought
Whence that high singer's rapture came.
—When now I turn the leaf the same
Immortal light illumes the lay,
But from the letters of her name
The radiance has waned away!

Weathers

This is the weather the cuckoo likes,
And so do I;
When showers betumble the chestnut spikes,
And nestlings fly;
And the little brown nightingale bills his best,
And they sit outside at 'The Traveller's Rest,'
And maids come forth sprig-muslin drest,
And citizens dream of the south and west,
And so do I.

This is the weather the shepherd shuns,
And so do I;
When beeches drip in browns and duns,
And thresh and ply;
And hill-hid tides throb, throe on throe,
And meadow rivulets overflow,
And drops on gate bars hang in a row,
And rooks in families homeward go,
And so do I.

HEINRICH HEINE
(1797–1856)

"Your eyes of azure violets"

Your eyes of azure violets,
Your cheeks of roses red,
Your delicate little hand
With lilies white outspread—
All blossom on forever,
And only your heart is dead.

"Ah, yes, my songs are poisoned"

Ah, yes, my songs are poisoned;
  How can this but be true,
When, in my bloom of life,
  You've given me this rue?
Ah yes, my songs are poisoned;
  How can this but be true,
When, in my heart nest vipers,
  And you, my love, and you.

"Beauteous, bright, and golden star"

Beauteous, bright, and golden star,
Greet my loved one from afar;
I am (This to her aver),
Heartsick, pale and bound to her.

"The runestone rises in the sea"

The runestone rises in the sea;
    There sit I dreaming today.
The wind doth whistle, the seagulls call,
    The waves all billow and play.

I have loved many fair-haired lads
    And many a maiden gay.
Where are they now? The wind doth whistle,
    The waves all billow and play.

THOMAS HOOD
(1799–1845)

The Bridge of Sighs

One more unfortunate,
    Weary of breath,
Rashly importunate,
    Gone to her death.

Take her up tenderly,
    Life her with care;
Fashion'd so slenderly,
    Young and so fair.

Look at her garments
    Clinging like cerements;
Whilst the wave constantly
    Drips from her clothing.
Take her up instantly,
    Loving, not loathing.

INDEPENDENT
BOOKSELLERS

★

M^cNALLY
JACKSON

★

TEL (212) 274-1160
52 PRINCE ST, NYC
M^cNALLYJACKSON.COM

FOR THOSE WHO HATE WRITING IN BOOKS

★ ★ ★ ★ ★ ★ ★

_____

_____

_____

_____

_____

_____

_____

_____

_____

★ ★ ★ ★ ★ ★ ★

GERARD MANLEY HOPKINS
(1844–1889)

Spring and Fall to a Young Child

Margaret, are you grieving
Over Goldengrove unleaving?
Leaves, like the things of man, you
With your fresh thoughts care for, can you?
Ah! as the heart grows older
It will come to such sights colder
By and by, nor spare a sigh
Though worlds of wanwood leafmeal lie;
And yet you will weep and know why.
Now no matter, child, the name:
Sorrow's springs are the same.
Nor mouth had, no nor mind, expressed
What heart heard of, ghost guessed:
It is the blight man was born for,
It is Margaret you mourn for.

A Nun Takes the Veil

I have desired to go
Where springs not fail,
To fields where flies no sharp and sided hail

And a few lilies blow.
I have desired to go.
And I have asked to be
Where no storms come,
Where the green swell is in the havens dumb,
And out of the swing of the sea.
I have asked to be.

I have desired to go
Where springs not fail,
To fields where flies no sharp and sided hail
And a few lilies blow.
I have desired to go.
And I have asked to be

Where no storms come,
Where the green swell is in the havens dumb,
And out of the swing of the sea.
I have asked to be.

Pied Beauty

Glory be to God for dappled things—
    For skies of couple-colour as a brinded cow;
        For rose-moles all in stipple upon trout that swim;
Fresh-firecoal chestnut-falls; finches' wings;
    Landscape plotted and pieced —fold, fallow, and plough;
        And áll trádes, their gear and tackle and trim.

All things counter, original, spare, strange;
    Whatever is fickle, freckled (who knows how?)
        With swift, slow; sweet, sour; adazzle, dim;
He fathers-forth whose beauty is past change:
            Praise him.

WILLIAM JAMES
(1842–1910)

"Hoggamus, higgamus"

Hoggamus, higgamus,
Men are polygamous.
Higgamus, hoggamus,
Women monogamous.

JOHN KEATS
(1795–1821)

Song

I had a dove and the sweet dove died;
And I have thought it died of grieving:
O, what could it grieve for? Its feet were tied,
With a silken thread of my own hand's weaving;
Sweet little red feet! why should you die—
Why should you leave me, sweet bird! why?
You lived alone in the forest-tree,
Why, pretty thing! would you not live with me?
I kiss'd you oft and gave you white peas;
Why not live sweetly, as in the green trees?

On First Looking into Chapman's Homer

Much have I traveled in the realms of gold,
And many goodly states and kingdoms seen;
Round many western islands have I been
Which bards in fealty to Apollo hold.
Oft of one wide expanse had I been told
That deep-browed Homer ruled as his demesne;
Yet did I never breathe its pure serene
Till I heard Chapman speak out loud and bold:
Then felt I like some watcher of the skies
When a new planet swims into his ken;
Or like stout Cortes when with eagle eyes
He stared at the Pacific—and all his men
Looked at each other with a wild surmise—
Silent, upon a peak in Darien.

Bright Star! Would I Were Steadfast As Thou Art

Bright star! would I were steadfast as thou art—
Not in lone splendor hung aloft the night
And watching, with eternal lids apart,
Like nature's patient, sleepless Eremite,
The moving waters at their priestlike task
Of pure ablution round earth's human shores,
Or gazing on the new soft-fallen mask
Of snow upon the mountains and the moors—
No—yet still stedfast, still unchangeable,
Pillowed upon my fair love's ripening breast,
To feel for ever its soft fall and swell,
Awake for ever in a sweet unrest,
Still, still to hear her tender-taken breath,
And so live ever—or else swoon to death.

ALPHONSE DE LAMARTINE
(1790–1869)

The book of Life is the final tome

The book of Life is the final tome
That we cannot open or close at will.
The passages there are read but once,
And the fatal leaves do not stand still.
To return to the page where we love we yearn,
But the page where we die is before us, to turn.

WALTER SAVAGE LANDOR
(1775–1864)

Ianthe

From you, Ianthe, little troubles pass
  Like little ripples down a sunny river;
Your pleasures spring like daisies in the grass,
  Cut down, and up again, as blithe as ever.

Ireland Never Was Contented

Ireland never was contented.
Say you so? You are demented.
Ireland was contented when
All could use the sword and pen.
And when Tara rose so high
That her turrets split the sky.
And about her courts were seen
Liveried angels robed in green,
Wearing, by St. Peter's bounty,
Emeralds big as half the county.

SIDNEY LANIER
(1842–1881)

The Stirrup-Cup

Death, thou'rt a cordial old and rare:
Look how compounded, with what care!
Time got his wrinkles reaping thee
Sweet herbs from all antiquity.

David to thy distillage went,
Keats, and Gotama excellent,
Omar Khayyam, and Chaucer bright,
And Shakespeare for a king-delight.

Then, Time, let not a drop be spilt:
Hand me the cup whene'er thou wilt;
'Tis thy rich stirrup-cup to me;
I'll drink it down right smilingly.

HENRY WADSWORTH LONGFELLOW
(1807–1882)

"The Tide Rises, the Tide Falls"

The tide rises, the tide falls,
The twilight darkens, the curlew calls;
Along the sea-sands damp and brown
The traveler hastens toward the town,
And the tide rises, the tide falls.
Darkness settles on roofs and walls,
But the sea, the sea in darkness calls;
The little waves, with their soft, white hands
Efface the footprints in the sands,
And the tide rises, the tide falls.
The morning breaks; the steeds in their stalls
Stamp and neigh, as the hostler calls;
The day returns, but nevermore
Returns the traveler to the shore.
And the tide rises, the tide falls.

Serenade from "The Spanish Student"

Stars of the summer night!
    Far in yon azure deeps,
Hide, hide your golden light!
    She sleeps!
My lady sleeps!
    Sleeps!

Moon of the summer night!
  Far down yon western steeps,
Sink, sink in silver light!
  She sleeps!
My lady sleeps!
  Sleeps!

Wind of the summer night!
  Where yonder woodbine creeps,
Fold, fold thy pinions light!
  She sleeps!
My lady sleeps!
  Sleeps!

Dreams of the summer night!
  Tell her, her lover keeps
Watch! while in slumbers light
  She sleeps!
My lady sleeps!
  Sleeps!

JAMES RUSSELL LOWELL
(1819–1891)

Monna Lisa

She gave me all that woman can,
Nor her soul's nunnery forego,
A confidence that man to man
Without remorse can never show.

Rare art, that can the sense refine
Till not a pulse rebellious stirs,
And, since she never can be mine,
Makes it seem sweeter to be hers!

HERMAN MELVILLE
(1819–1891)

Art

In placid hours well-pleased we dream
Of many a brave unbodied scheme.
But form to lend, pulsed life create,
What unlike things must meet and mate:
A flame to melt—a wind to freeze;

Sad patience—joyous energies;
Humility—yet pride and scorn;
Instinct and study; love and hate;
Audacity—reverence. These must mate,
And fuse with Jacob's mystic heart,
To wrestle with the angel—Art.

GEORGE MEREDITH
(1828–1909)

"They have no song, the sedges dry"

They have no song, the sedges dry,
    And still they sing.
It is within my breast they sing,
    As I pass by.
Within my breast they touch a string,
    They wake a sigh.
There is but sound of sedges dry;
    In me they sing.

Dirge in Woods

And below

Not a breath of wild air;
Still as the mosses that glow
On the flooring and over the lines
Of the roots here and there.
The pine-tree drops its dead;
They are quiet, as under the sea.
Overhead, overhead
Rushes life in a race,
As the clouds the clouds chase;

And we go,
And we drop like the fruits of the tree,

Even we,

Even so.

ALICE MEYNELL
(1847–1922)

Chimes

Brief, on a flying night,
From the shaken tower,
A flock of bells take flight,
And go with the hour.

Like birds from the cote to the gales,
Abrupt—O hark!
A fleet of bells set sails,
And go to the dark.

Sudden the cold airs swing.
Alone, aloud,
A verse of bells takes wing
And flies with the cloud.

COVENTRY PATMORE
(1823–1896)

The Foreign Land

A woman is a foreign land,
Of which, though there he settle young,
A man will ne'er quite understand
The customs, politics, and tongue.
The foolish hie them post-haste through,
See fashions odd, and prospects fair,
Learn of the language, "How d'ye do,"
And go and brag they have been there.
The most for leave to trade apply,
For once, at Empire's seat, her heart,
Then get what knowledge ear and eye
Glean chancewise in the life-long mart.
And certain others, few and fit,
Attach them to the Court, and see
The Country's best, its accent hit,
And partly sound its polity.

EDGAR ALLAN POE
(1809–1849)

To Helen

Helen, thy beauty is to me
 Like those Nicèan barks of yore
That gently, o'er a perfumed sea,
 The weary way-worn wanderer bore
 To his own native shore.

On desperate seas long wont to roam,
 Thy hyacinth hair, thy classic face,
Thy Naiad airs have brought me home
 To the glory that was Greece,
And the grandeur that was Rome.

Lo, in yon brilliant window-niche
  How statue-like I see thee stand,
  The agate lamp within thy hand,
Ah! Psyche, from the regions which
  Are holy land!

ALEXANDER PUSHKIN
(1799–1837)

I Loved You ("_ ___ _____")

Loved you, I did, may even love you still;
My heart's fire's not cold:
But don't let that bother you;
I've no wish to sadden you at all.
I loved you wordlessly, hopelessly,
Tormented so by jealousy.
Loved you, I did, so truly, so dearly:
Let God grant you another such love.

—*Translated from the Russian by Bob Blaisdell*

CHRISTINA ROSSETTI
(1830–1894)

A Birthday

My heart is like a singing bird
  Whose nest is in a water'd shoot;
My heart is like an apple-tree
  Whose boughs are bent with thick-set fruit;
My heart is like a rainbow shell
  That paddles in a halcyon sea;
My heart is gladder than all these,
  Because my love is come to me.

Raise me a daïs of silk and down;
    Hang it with vair and purple dyes;
Carve it in doves and pomegranates,
    And peacocks with a hundred eyes;
Work it in gold and silver grapes,
    In leaves and silver fleurs-de-lys;
Because the birthday of my life
    Is come, my love is come to me.

DANTE GABRIEL ROSSETTI
(1828–1882)

Silent Noon

Your hands lie open in the long fresh grass,—
The finger-points look through like rosy blooms:
Your eyes smile peace. The pasture gleams and glooms
'Neath billowing skies that scatter and amass.
All round our nest, far as the eye can pass,
Are golden kingcup-fields with silver edge
Where the cow-parsley skirts the hawthorn-hedge.
'Tis visible silence, still as the hour-glass.

Deep in the sun-search'd growths the dragon-fly
Hangs like a blue thread loosen'd from the sky:—
So this wing'd hour is dropt to us from above.
Oh! clasp we to our hearts, for deathless dower,
This close-companion'd inarticulate hour
When twofold silence was the song of love.

PERCY BYSSHE SHELLEY
(1792–1822)

Rome and Nature

Rome has fallen, ye see it lying
Heaped in undistinguished ruin:
Nature is alone undying.

To _____

Music when soft voices die,
Vibrates in the memory
Odours when sweet violets sicken,
Live within the sense they quicken.

Rose leaves, when the rose is dead,
Are heaped for the beloved bed;
And so thy thoughts, when thou art gone,
Love itself shall slumber on.

A Lament

O world! O Life! O Time!
On whose last steps I climb,
   Trembling at that where I had stood before;
When will return the glory of your prime?
   No more—O nevermore!
Out of the day and night
A joy has taken flight:
   Fresh spring, and summer, and winter hoar,
Move my faint heart with grief, but with delight
   No more—O nevermore!

A Dirge

Rough wind that moanest loud,
   Grief too sad for song;
Wild wind when sullen cloud
   Knells all the night long;
Sad storm, whose tears are vain,
Bare woods whose branches strain,
Deep caves and dreary main,
   Wail! for the world's wrong!

ROBERT LOUIS STEVENSON
(1850–1894)

My Wife

Trusty, dusky, vivid, true,
With eyes of gold and bramble-dew,
Steel-true and blade-straight,
The great artificer
Made my mate.

Honour, anger, valour, fire;
A love that life could never tire,
Death quench or evil stir,
The mighty master
Gave to her.

Teacher, tender, comrade, wife,
A fellow-farer true through life,
Heart-whole and soul-free
The august father
Gave to me.

Happy Thought

The world is so full of a number of things,
I'm sure we should all be as happy as kings.

Envoy

Go, little book, and wish to all
Flowers in the garden, meat in the hall,
A bin of wine, a spice of wit,
A house with lawns enclosing it,
A living river by the door,
A nightingale in the sycamore!

THEODOR STORM
(1817–1888)

"Only for Today"

Only for today
    Am I so gay.
Tomorrow all of this
    Will fade away.

Only for this hour
    Are you my own.
I know I must die, joyless,
    And all alone.

ARTHUR SYMONS
(1865–1945)

During Music

The music had the heat of blood,
A passion that no words can reach;
We sat together, and understood
Our own heart's speech.

We had no need of word or sign,
The music spoke for us, and said
All that her eyes could read in mine
Or mine in hers had read.

JOHN BANISTER TABB
(1845–1909)

Holy Ground

Pause, where apart the fallen sparrow lies,
  And lightly tread;
For there the pity of a Father's eyes
  Enshrines the dead.

Influences

Each separate life is fed
From many a fountainhead;
Tides that we never know
Into our being flow,
And rays of the remotest star
Converge to make us what we are.

Fern Song

Dance to the beat of the rain, little Fern,
And spread out your palms again,
And say, "Tho' the sun
Hath my vesture spun,
He had labored, alas, in vain,
But for the shade
That the Cloud hath made,
And the gift of the Dew and the Rain."
Then laugh and upturn
All your fronds, little Fern,
And rejoice in the beat of the rain!

ALFRED, LORD TENNYSON
(1809–1892)

"Sweet and Low"

Sweet and low, sweet and low,
Wind of the western sea,
Low, low, breathe and blow,
Wind of the western sea!
Over the rolling waters go,
Come from the dying moon, and blow,
Blow him again to me;
While my little one, while my pretty one, sleeps.

Sleep and rest, sleep and rest,
Father will come to thee soon;
Rest, rest, on mother's breast,
Father will come to thee soon;
Father will come to his babe in the nest,
Silver sails all out of the west
Under the silver moon:
Sleep, my little one, sleep, my pretty one, sleep.

The Beggar Maid

Her arms across her breast she laid;
She was more fair than words can say:
Bare-footed came the beggar maid
Before the king Cophetua.
In robe and crown the king stept down,
To meet and greet her on her way;
"It is no wonder," said the lords,
"She is more beautiful than day."

As shines the moon in clouded skies,
She in her poor attire was seen:
One praised her ancles, one her eyes,
One her dark hair and lovesome mien:

So sweet a face, such angel grace,
In all that land had never been:
Cophetua sware a royal oath:
"This beggar maid shall be my queen!"

"Home They Brought Her Warrior Dead"

Home they brought her warrior dead:
She nor swooned, nor uttered cry:
All her maidens, watching, said,
'She must weep or she will die.'

Then they praised him, soft and low,
Called him worthy to be loved,
Truest friend and noblest foe;
Yet she neither spoke nor moved.

Stole a maiden from her place,
Lightly to the warrior stepped,
Took the face-cloth from the face;
Yet she neither moved nor wept.

Rose a nurse of ninety years,
Set his child upon her knee—
Like summer tempest came her tears—
'Sweet my child, I live for thee.'

WILLIAM M. THACKERAY
(1811–1863)

The Sorrows of Werther

Werther had a love for Charlotte
Such as words could never utter;
Would you know how first he met her?
She was cutting bread and butter.

Charlotte was a married lady,
And a moral man was Werther,
And, for all the wealth of Indies,
Would do nothing for to hurt her.

So he sighed and pined and ogled,
And his passion boiled and bubbled,
Till he blew his silly brains out,
And no more by it was troubled.

Charlotte, having seen his body
Borne before her on a shutter,
Like a well-conducted person,
Went on cutting bread and butter.

EDWARD THOMAS
(1878–1917)

Thaw

Over the land freckled with snow half-thawed
The speculating rooks at their nests cawed,
And saw from elm-tops, delicate as flower of grass,
What we below could not see, Winter pass.

FRANCIS THOMPSON
(1859–1907)

Envoy

Go, songs, for ended is our brief, sweet play;
Go, children of swift joy and tardy sorrow:
And some are sung, and that was yesterday,
And some unsung, and that may be tomorrow.

Go forth; and if it be o'er stony way,
Old joy can lend what newer grief must borrow:
And it was sweet, and that was yesterday,
And sweet is sweet, though purchased with sorrow.

Go, songs, and come not back from your far way:
And if men ask you why ye smile and sorrow,
Tell them ye grieve, for your hearts know today,
Tell them ye smile, for your eyes know tomorrow.

HENRY DAVID THOREAU
(1817–1862)

Mist

Low-anchored cloud,
Newfoundland air,
Fountain-head and source of rivers,
Dew-cloth, dream-drapery,
And napkin spread by fays;
Drifting meadow of the air,
Where bloom the daisied banks and violets,
And in whose fenny labyrinth
The bittern booms and heron wades;
Spirit of lakes and seas and rivers,
Bear only perfumes and the scent
Of healing herbs to just men's fields!

Rumors from an Aeolian Harp

There is a vale which none hath seen,
Where foot of man has never been,
Such as here lives with toil and strife,
An anxious and a sinful life.
There every virtue has its birth,
Ere it descends upon the earth,
And thither every deed returns,
Which in the generous bosom burns.

There love is warm, and youth is young,
And poetry is yet unsung.
For Virtue still adventures there,
And freely breathes her native air.

And ever, if you hearken well,
You still may hear its vesper bell,
And tread of high-souled men go by,
Their thoughts conversing with the sky.

FREDERICK G. TUCKERMAN
(1821–1873)

And Two I Knew

And two I knew, an old man and a boy,
Alternate helpers: for their day was spent
In gathering forest bark; and when they went
Late home, the elder did his time employ
To teach the other, and tell him what he knew
Of history, myth, or mathematics hard,
In hours of night, and when the night was dark,
Showed him Job's Coffin and the Golden Yard,
Showed the nine moonstars in the moonless blue,
And the great Circle of the Bestiary;
So that the child grew up to love the sky
And, in the woods beyond the hemlock bark,
To heed the intricate moss that o'er it grew,
The shadowy flower all wet with all-day dew.

PAUL VERLAINE
(1844–1896)

"It weeps in my heart"

It weeps in my heart,
    As it rains on the town.
What tears me apart?
    What sorrow of heart?

O sweet sound of the rain,
  On the roofs, on the pane.
For a heart that has grief,
  O the sound of the rain!

It weeps without reason
  Within my sad heart;
What? No awful treason?
  This gloom has no reason.

'Tis such a dread weight,
  Not to comprehend why,
Without love, without hate,
  My heart bears such weight.

The Song of Gaspar Hauser

An orphan, with tranquil eyes,
  To the cities I made my way,
To mingle with men of the day;
  They did not find me wise.

At twenty a new unrest
  Set my heart and soul afire;
For women I had desire.
  They did not welcome my quest.

Although I chanced to be
  Sans country, sans king, barely brave,
My life to war's throes I gave.
  Death wished no part of me.

Was I born too soon or too late?
  WHY am I here in this life?
With pain my existence is rife.
  O, all of you, pray for my fate!

Autumn Song

The wailings of Autumn's
    Violins
Pierce through my heart,
    Where dull languor begins.

All pale and wan,
    As when tolls the bell,
I think of the past,
    And I weep for its knell.

And I go, as the wind
    Carries me ahead,
Straying here, straying there,
    Like a leaf that is dead.

JONES VERY
(1813–1880)

The Light from Within

I saw on earth another light
Than that which lit my eye
Come forth as from my soul within,
And from a higher sky.

Its beams shone still unclouded on,
When in the farthest west
The sun I once had known had sunk
Forever to his rest.

And on I walked, though dark the night,
Nor rose his orb by day;
As one who by a surer guide
Was pointed out the way.

'Twas brighter far than noonday's beam;
It shone from God within,
And lit, as by a lamp from heaven,
The world's dark track of sin.

WILLIAM WATSON
(1858–1935)

Song

April, April,
Laugh thy girlish laughter;
Then, the moment after,
Weep thy girlish tears!
April, that mine ears
Like a lover greetest,
If I tell thee, sweetest,
All my hopes and fears,
April, April,
Laugh thy golden laughter,
But, the moment after,
Weep thy golden tears!

Epigram

The poet gathers fruit from every tree,
Yea, grapes from thorns and figs from thistles he,
Pluck'd by his hand, the basest weed that grows
Towers to a lily, reddens to a rose.

WALT WHITMAN
(1819–1892)

"When I Heard the Learn'd Astronomer"

When I heard the learn'd astronomer,
When the proofs, the figures, were ranged in columns before me,
When I was shown the charts, the diagrams, to add, divide,
    and measure them,
When I sitting heard the learned astronomer where he lectured
    with much applause in the lecture room,

How soon unaccountable I became tired and sick,
Till rising and gliding out I wander'd off by myself,
In the mystical moist night-air, and from time to time,
Look'd up in perfect silence at the stars.

"I hear it was charged against me that I sought to destroy institutions"

I hear it was charged against me that I sought to
    destroy institutions;
But really I am neither for nor against institutions;
(What indeed have I in common with them?—Or what with
    the destruction of them?)
Only I will establish in the Mannahatta, and in every city of
    These States, inland and seaboard,
And in the fields and woods, and above every keel, little or
    large, that dents the water,
Without edifices, or rules, or trustees, or any argument,
The institution of the dear love of comrades.

The Last Invocation

1
At the last, tenderly,
From the walls of the powerful, fortress'd house,
From the clasp of the knitted locks—from the keep of
    the well-closed doors,
Let me be wafted.

2
Let me glide noiselessly forth;
With the key of softness unlock the locks—with a whisper,
Set ope the doors, O Soul!

3
Tenderly! be not impatient!
(Strong is your hold, O mortal flesh!
Strong is your hold, O love.)

WILLIAM WORDSWORTH
(1770–1850)

A Slumber Did My Spirit Seal

A slumber did my spirit seal;
  I had no human fears;
She seemed a thing that could not feel
  The touch of earthly years.

No motion has she now, no force;
  She neither hears nor sees;
Rolled round in earth's diurnal course,
  With rocks, and stones, and trees.

The World Is Too Much with Us

The world is too much with us; late and soon,
Getting and spending, we lay waste our powers;
Little we see in Nature that is ours;
We have given our hearts away, a sordid boon!
This Sea that bares her bosom to the moon,
The winds that will be howling at all hours,
And are up-gathered now like sleeping flowers,
For this, for everything, we are out of tune;
It moves us not.—Great God! I'd rather be
A Pagan suckled in a creed outworn;
So might I, standing on this pleasant lea,
Have glimpses that would make me less forlorn;
Have sight of Proteus rising from the sea;
Or hear old Triton blow his wreathèd horn.

London, 1802

Milton! thou should'st be living at this hour:
England hath need of thee: she is a fen
Of stagnant waters: altar, sword, and pen,
Fireside, the heroic wealth of hall and bower,
Have forfeited their ancient English dower
Of inward happiness. We are selfish men;
Oh! raise us up, return to us again;
And give us manners, virtue, freedom, power.
Thy soul was like a Star, and dwelt apart:
Thou hadst a voice whose sound was like the sea:
Pure as the naked heavens, majestic, free,
So didst thou travel on life's common way,
In cheerful godliness; and yet thy heart
The lowliest duties on herself did lay.

Composed upon Westminster Bridge

Earth has not anything to show more fair:
Dull would he be of soul who could pass by
A sight so touching in its majesty:
This City now doth, like a garment, wear
The beauty of the morning; silent, bare,
Ships, towers, domes, theatres, and temples lie
Open unto the fields, and to the sky;
All bright and glittering in the smokeless air.
Never did sun more beautifully steep
In his first splendor, valley, rock, or hill;
Ne'er saw I, never felt, a calm so deep!
The river glideth at his own sweet will:
Dear God! the very houses seem asleep;
And all that mighty heart is lying still!

To a Skylark

Ethereal minstrel! pilgrim of the sky!
Dost thou despise the earth where cares abound?
Or, while the wings aspire, are heart and eye
Both with thy nest upon the dewy ground?
Thy nest which thou canst drop into at will,
Those quivering wings composed, that music still!
Leave to the nightingale her shady wood;
A privacy of glorious light is thine;
Whence thou dost pour upon the world a flood
Of harmony, with instinct more divine;
Type of the wise who soar, but never roam;
True to the kindred points of Heaven and Home!

Twentieth Century

RICHARD ALDINGTON
(1892–1962)

Evening

The chimneys, rank on rank,
Cut the clear sky;
The moon
With a rag of gauze about her loins
Poses among them, an awkward Venus—

And here am I looking wantonly at her
Over the kitchen sink.

Image

Like a gondola of green scented fruits,
Drifting along the dank canals of Venice,
You, O exquisite one,
Have entered into my desolate city.

ANONYMOUS (Japanese)

"If only when one heard"

If only when one heard
That Old Age was coming,
One could bolt the door,
Answer "Not at home,"
And refuse to meet him!

GUILLAUME APOLLINAIRE
(1880–1918)

The Sirens

Do I know, oh Sirens,
    Whence comes your ennui,
As you sing in the night
    Your songs that bring tears?
I am full of voices,
    Like you, oh sea,
And my vessels that sing
    Are called the years.

Crayfish
(L'écrevisse)

In certitude, oh my delight,
You and I, we share this plight:
We move like crayfish of the ocean,
In ever backward, backward motion.

HILAIRE BELLOC
(1870–1953)

Epitaph on the Politician Himself

Here richly, with ridiculous display,
The Politician's corpse was laid away.
While all of his acquaintance sneered and slanged,
I wept: for I had longed to see him hanged.

BERTOLT BRECHT
(1898–1956)

The Mask of Evil

On my wall hangs a Japanese carving,
The mask of an evil demon, decorated with gold lacquer.
Sympathetically I observe
The swollen veins of the forehead, indicating
What a strain it is to be evil.

—*Translated by H. R. Hays*

WITTER BYNNER
(1881–1968)

"If I were only dafter"

If I were only dafter
    I might be making hymns
To the liquor of your laughter
    And the lacquer of your limbs.

JOSEPH CAMPBELL
(1879–1944)

The Old Woman

As a white candle
In a holy place,
So is the beauty
Of an aged face.

As the spent radiance
Of the winter sun,
So is a woman
With her travail done.

Her brood gone from her
And her thoughts as still
As the waters
Under a ruined mill.

ADELAIDE CRAPSEY
(1878–1914)

Susanna and the Elders

"Why do
You so devise
Evil against her?" "For that
She is beautiful, delicate;
Therefore."

Niagara
(seen on a night in November)

How frail
Above the bulk
Of crashing water hangs,
Autumnal, evanescent, wan,
The moon.

These Be Three Silent Things

These be
Three silent things:
The falling snow, the hour
Before the dawn, the mouth of one
Just dead.

ROBERT CREELEY
(1926–2005)

After Lorca

        The church is a business, and the rich
are the business men.
                When they pull on the bells, the
poor come piling in and when a poor man dies, he has a wooden
cross, and they rush through the ceremony.

But when a rich man dies, they
drag out the Sacrament
and a golden Cross, and go *doucement, doucement*
to the cemetery.

And the poor love it
and think it's crazy.

WALTER DE LA MARE
(1873–1956)

An Epitaph

Here lies a most beautiful lady,
Light of step and heart was she;
I think she was the most beautiful lady
That ever was in the West Country.

But beauty vanishes; beauty passes;
However rare—rare it be;
And when I crumble, who will remember
This lady of the West Country?

H.D. [HILDA DOOLITTLE]
(1886–1961)

Song

You are as gold
As the half-ripe grain
That merges to gold again,
As white as the white rain
That beats through
The half-opened flowers
Of the great flower tufts
Thick on the black limbs
Of an Illyrian apple bough.

Can honey distill such fragrance
As your bright hair?—
For your face is as fair as rain,
Yet as rain that lies clear
On white honey-comb,
Lends radiance to the white wax,
So your hair on your brow
Casts light for a shadow.

JOHN DRINKWATER
(1882–1937)

Birthright

Lord Rameses of Egypt sighed
   Because a summer evening passed;
And little Ariadne cried
   That summer fancy fell at last
To dust; and young Verona died
   When beauty's hour was overcast.

Theirs was the bitterness we know
   Because the clouds of hawthorn keep
So short a state, and kisses go
   To tombs unfathomably deep,
While Rameses and Romeo
   And little Ariadne sleep.

LORD DUNSANY
(1878–1957)

To Keats

On a magical morning, with twinkling feet,
And a song at his lips that was strange and sweet,
Somebody new came down the street
To the world's derision and laughter.

Now he is dumb with no more to say,
Now he is dead and taken away,
Silent and still and leading the way,
And the world comes tumbling after.

T. S. ELIOT
(1888–1965)

Morning at the Window

They are rattling breakfast plates in basement kitchens,
And along the trampled edges of the street
I am aware of the damp souls of housemaids
Sprouting despondently at area gates.

The brown waves of fog toss up to me
Twisted faces from the bottom of the street,
And tear from a passer-by with muddy skirts
An aimless smile that hovers in the air
And vanishes along the level of the roofs.

Aunt Helen

Miss Helen Slingsby was my maiden aunt,
And lived in a small house near a fashionable square
Cared for by servants to the number of four.
Now when she died there was silence in heaven
And silence at her end of the street.
The shutters were drawn and the undertaker wiped his feet—
He was aware that this sort of thing had occurred before.
The dogs were handsomely provided for,
But shortly afterwards the parrot died too.
The Dresden clock continued ticking on the mantelpiece,
And the footman sat upon the dining-table
Holding the second housemaid on his knees—
Who had always been so careful while her mistress lived.

Cousin Nancy

Miss Nancy Ellicott
Strode across the hills and broke them,
Rode across the hills and broke them—
The barren New England hills—
Riding to hounds
Over the cow-pasture.

Miss Nancy Ellicott smoked
And danced all the modern dances;
And her aunts were not quite sure how they felt about it,
But they knew that it was modern.

Upon the glazen shelves kept watch
Matthew and Waldo, guardians of the faith,
The army of unalterable law.

MARTÍN ESPADA
(b. 1957)

Confessions of the Tenant in Apt. #2

The landlord's beige
Fleetwood Cadillac
died in front of the building;
and I was secretly happy
that my jumper cables
didn't work.

JOHN GOULD FLETCHER
(1886–1950)

The Skaters

Black swallows swooping or gliding
In a flurry of entangled loops and curves;
The skaters skim over the frozen river.
And the grinding click of their skates
    as they impinge upon the surface,
Is like the brushing together of thin wing-tips of silver.

F. S. FLINT
(1885–1960)

Houses

Evening and quiet:
a bird trills in the poplar trees
behind the house with the dark green door
across the road.

Into the sky,
the red earthenware and the galvanised iron chimneys
thrust their cowls.
The hoot of the steamers on the Thames is plain.

No wind;
the trees merge, green with green;
a car whirs by;
footsteps and voices take their pitch
in the key of dusk,
far-off and near, subdued.

Solid and square to the world
the houses stand,
their windows blocked with venetian blinds.

Nothing will move them.

ROBERT FROST
(1874–1963)

Dust of Snow

The way a crow
Shook down on me
The dust of snow
From a hemlock tree

Has given my heart
A change of mood
And saved some part
Of a day I had rued.

Nothing Gold Can Stay

Nature's first green is gold,
Her hardest hue to hold.
Her early leaf's a flower;
But only so an hour.
Then leaf subsides to leaf.
So Eden sank to grief,
So dawn goes down to day.
Nothing gold can stay.

The Lesson For Today

And were an epitaph to be my story
I'd have a short one ready for my own.
I would have written of me on my stone:
I had a lover's quarrel with the world.

Fire and Ice

Some say the world will end in fire,
Some say in ice.
From what I've tasted of desire
I hold with those who favor fire.
But if it had to perish twice,
I think I know enough of hate
To say that for destruction ice
Is also great
And would suffice.

A. E. HOUSMAN
(1859–1936)

"When I Would Muse in Boyhood"

When I would muse in boyhood
    The wild green woods among,
And nurse resolves and fancies
    Because the world was young,
It was not foes to conquer,
    Nor sweethearts to be kind,
But it was friends to die for
    That I would seek and find.

I sought them far and found them,
    The sure, the straight, the brave,
The hearts I lost my own to,
    The souls I could not save.
They braced their belts about them,
    They crossed in ships the sea,
They sought and found six feet of ground,
    And there they died for me.

LANGSTON HUGHES
(1902–1967)

Personal

In an envelope marked:
PERSONAL
God addressed me a letter.
In an envelope marked:
PERSONAL
I have given my answer.

T. E. HULME
(1883–1917)

Autumn

A touch of cold in the Autumn night—
I walked abroad,
And saw the ruddy moon lean over a hedge
Like a red-faced farmer.
I did not stop to speak, but nodded;
And round about were the wistful stars
With white faces like town children.

MAX JACOB
(1876–1944)

Villanelle

O tell me what was the song
    Sung by the Sirens fair,
    To lure into their lair
Greek triremes that sailed along?

JAMES JOYCE
(1882–1941)

I Hear an Army

I hear an army charging upon the land,
  And the thunder of horses plunging, foam about their knees.
Arrogant, in black armour, behind them stand,
  Disdaining the reins, with fluttering whips, the charioteers.

They cry unto the night their battle-name:
  I moan in sleep when I hear afar their whirling laughter.
They cleave the gloom of dreams, a blinding flame,
  Clanging, clanging upon the heart as upon an anvil.

They come shaking in triumph their long, green hair:
  They come out of the sea and run shouting by the shore.
My heart, have you no wisdom thus to despair?
  My love, my love, my love, why have you left me alone?

FRANZ KAFKA
(1883–1924)

The Sirens

These are the seductive voices of the night.
The Sirens sang that way.
I would be doing them an injustice to think
    that they wanted to seduce.
They knew they had claws and sterile wombs,
And they lamented this aloud.
They could not help it if their laments sounded so beautiful.

ALFRED KREYMBORG
(1883–1966)

Clay

I wish
there were thirteen
gods in the sky,
even twelve might achieve it:

Or even
one god
in me:

Alone,
I can't shape
an image of her.

D. H. LAWRENCE
(1885–1930)

Aware

Slowly the moon is rising out of the ruddy haze,
Divesting herself of her golden shift, and so
Emerging white and exquisite; and I in amaze
See in the sky before me, a woman I did not know
I loved, but there she goes and her beauty hurts my heart;
I follow her down the night, begging her not to depart.

Nonentity

The stars that open and shut
Fall on my shallow breast
Like stars on a pool.

The soft wind, blowing cool
Laps little crest after crest
Of ripples across my breast.

And dark grass under my feet
Seems to dabble in me
Like grass in a brook.

Oh, and it is sweet
To be all these things, not to be
Any more myself.

For look,
I am weary of myself!

Change

Do you think it is easy to change?
Ah, it is very hard to change and be different.
It means passing through the waters of oblivion.

VACHEL LINDSAY
(1879–1931)

Factory Windows Are Always Broken

Factory windows are always broken.
Somebody's always throwing bricks,
Somebody's always heaving cinders,
Playing ugly Yahoo tricks.

Factory windows are always broken.
Other windows are let alone.
No one throws through the chapel-window
The bitter, snarling, derisive stone.

Factory windows are always broken.
Something or other is going wrong.
Something is rotten—I think, in Denmark.
End of the factory-window song.

Euclid

Old Euclid drew a circle
On a sand-beach long ago.
He bounded and enclosed it
With angles thus and so.
His set of solemn greybeards
Nodded and argued much
Of arc and circumference,
Diameter and such.
A silent child stood by them
From morning until noon
Because they drew such charming
Round pictures of the moon.

AMY LOWELL
(1874–1925)

The Taxi

When I go away from you
The world beats dead
Like a slackened drum.
I call out for you against the jutted stars
And shout into the ridges of the wind.
Streets coming fast,
One after the other,
Wedge you away from me,
And the lamps of the city prick my eyes
So that I can no longer see your face.
Why should I leave you,
To wound myself upon the sharp edges of the night?

EDWIN MARKHAM
(1852–1940)

Outwitted

He drew a circle that shut me out—
Heretic, rebel, a thing to flout.
But Love and I had the wit to win:
We drew a circle that took him in!

JOHN MASEFIELD
(1878–1967)

Cargoes

Quinquireme of Nineveh from distant Ophir,
Rowing home to haven in sunny Palestine,
With a cargo of ivory,
And apes and peacocks,
Sandalwood, cedarwood, and sweet white wine.

Stately Spanish galleon coming from the Isthmus,
Dipping through the Tropics by the palm-green shores,
With a cargo of diamonds,
Emeralds, amethysts,
Topazes, and cinnamon, and gold moidores.

Dirty British coaster with a salt-caked smoke stack,
Butting through the Channel in the mad March days,
With a cargo of Tyne coal,
Road-rails, pig-lead,
Firewood, iron-ware, and cheap tin trays.

VIOLA MEYNELL
(1885–1956)

Dusting

The dust comes secretly day after day,
Lies on my ledge and dulls my shining things.
But O this dust I shall drive away
              Is flowers and kings,
Is Solomon's temple, poets, Nineveh.

EDNA ST. VINCENT MILLAY
(1892–1950)

Second Fig

Safe upon the solid rock
The ugly houses stand:
Come and see my shining palace
Built upon the sand!

Eel-Grass

No matter what I say,
   All that I really love
Is the rain that flattens on the bay,
   And the eel-grass in the cove;
The jingle-shells that lie and bleach
   At the tide-line, and the trace
Of higher tides along the beach:
   Nothing in this place.

Humoresque

"Heaven bless the babe!" they said.
"What queer books she must have read!"
(Love, by whom I was beguiled,
Grant I may not bear a child.)

"Little does she guess to-day
What the world may be!" they say.
(Snow, drift deep and cover
Till the spring my murdered lover.)

MARIANNE MOORE
(1887–1972)

I May, I Might, I Must

If you tell me why the fen
appears impassable, I then
will tell you why I think that I
can get across it if I try.

CHRISTOPHER MORLEY
(1890–1957)

Prudence

Help! Mad Dog! cried someone.
I hastened swiftly
In the opposite direction.
Wisdom, I murmured,
Is better than rabies.

DOROTHY PARKER
(1893–1967)

Sweet Violets

You are brief and frail and blue—
Little sister, I am too.
You are Heaven's masterpieces—
Little loves, the likeness ceases.

OCTAVIO PAZ
(1914–1998)

Touch ("Palpar")

My hands draw the curtains of you
Cover you in another nakedness
Discover the bodies of your body
My hands
create another body of your body.

—*Translated from the Spanish by Bob Blaisdell*

EZRA POUND
(1885–1972)

Alba

As cool as the pale wet leaves
Of lily-of-the-valley
She lay beside me in the dawn.

Chanson Arabe

I have shaken with love half the night
The winter rain falls in the street
She is but half my age;
Whither, whither am I going?
I have shaken with love half the night.
She is but half my age.
Whither, whither am I going?

JACQUES PRÉVERT
(1900–1977)

The Great Man

We met at the tailor
Of stone, who would take
His measurements down,
For posterity's sake.

RAINER MARIA RILKE
(1875–1926)

The Panther
In the Jardin des Plantes, Paris

From walking past the bars his eyes
have grown so tired, they retain nothing more.
It seems to him there are a thousand bars
and, behind those thousand bars, no world.

His soft walk, with lithe and strong steps,
turning in the smallest possible circle,
is like a dance of force around a midpoint
in which a mighty will stands benumbed.

Only at times is the curtain of his pupils
noiselessly raised. —Then an image enters,
passes through the tensed calm of his limbs—
and in his heart ceases to be.

—Translated from the German by Stanley Appelbaum

THEODORE ROETHKE
(1908–1963)

Heard in a Violent Ward

In heaven too,
You'd be institutionalized.
But that's all right,—
If they let you eat and swear
With the likes of Blake
And Christopher Smart,
And that sweet man John Clare.

CARL SANDBURG (1878–1967)

Playthings of the Wind
"The past is a bucket of ashes"

The woman named Tomorrow
sits with a hairpin in her teeth
and takes her time,
and does her hair the way she wants it,
and fastens at last the last braid and coil,
and puts the hairpin where it belongs,
and turns and drawls: Well, what of it?
My grandmother, Yesterday, is gone.
What of it? Let the dead be dead.

Fire-Logs

Nancy Hanks dreams by the fire;
Dreams, and the logs sputter,
And the yellow tongues climb.
Red lines lick their way in flickers.

Oh, sputter, logs.
    Oh, dream, Nancy.
Time now for a beautiful child.
Time now for a tall man to come.

Look at Six Eggs

Look at six eggs
In a mockingbird's nest.
Listen to six mockingbirds
Flinging follies of O-be-joyful
Over the marshes and uplands.
Look at songs,
Hidden in eggs.

Fog

The fog comes
on little cat feet.
It sits looking
over harbor and city
on silent haunches
and then moves on.

SIEGFRIED SASSOON
(1886–1967)

Everyone Sang

Everyone suddenly burst out singing;
And I was filled with such delight
As prisoned birds must find in freedom,
Winging wildly across the white
Orchards and dark-green fields; on—on—and out of sight.
Everyone's voice was suddenly lifted;

And beauty came like the setting sun:
My heart was shaken with tears; and horror
Drifted away . . . O, but Everyone
Was a bird; and the song was wordless;
   the singing will never be done.

GERTRUDE STEIN
(1874–1946)

I Am Rose

I am Rose; my eyes are blue
I am Rose and who are you
I am Rose and when I sing
I am Rose like anything.

WALLACE STEVENS
(1879–1955)

Disillusionment of Ten O'Clock

The houses are haunted
By white night-gowns.
None are green,
Or purple with green rings,
Or green with yellow rings,
Or yellow with blue rings.
None of them are strange,
With socks of lace
And beaded ceintures.
People are not going
To dream of baboons and periwinkles.
Only, here and there, an old sailor,
Drunk and asleep in his boots,
Catches tigers
In red weather.

The Wind Shifts

This is how the wind shifts:
Like the thoughts of an old human,
Who still thinks eagerly
And despairingly.
The wind shifts like this:
Like a human without illusions,
Who still feels irrational things within her.
The wind shifts like this:
Like humans approaching proudly,
Like humans approaching angrily.
This is how the wind shifts:
Like a human, heavy and heavy,
Who does not care.

SARA TEASDALE
(1884–1933)

The Look

Strephon kissed me in the spring,
Robin in the fall,
But Colin only looked at me
And never kissed at all.

Strephon's kiss was lost in jest,
Robin's lost in play,
But the kiss in Colin's eyes
Haunts me night and day.

Longing

I am not sorry for my soul
That it must go unsatisfied,
For it can live a thousand times,
Eternity is deep and wide.

I am not sorry for my soul,
But oh, my body that must go
Back to a little drift of dust
Without the joy it longed to know.

DYLAN THOMAS
(1914–1953)

The Hand That Signed the Paper

The hand that signed the paper felled a city;
Five sovereign fingers taxed the breath,
Doubled the globe of dead and halved a country;
These five kings did a king to death.

The mighty hand leads to a sloping shoulder,
The finger joints are cramped with chalk;
A goose's quill has put an end to murder
That put an end to talk.

The hand that signed the treaty bred a fever,
And famine grew, and locusts came;
Great is the hand that holds dominion over
Man by a scribbled name.

The five kings count the dead but do not soften
The crusted wound nor pat the brow;
A hand rules pity as a hand rules heaven;
Hands have no tears to flow.

WILLIAM CARLOS WILLIAMS
(1883–1963)

Willow Poem

It is a willow when summer is over,
a willow by the river
from which no leaf has fallen nor
bitten by the sun

turned orange or crimson.
The leaves cling and grow paler,
swing and grow paler
over the swirling waters of the river
as if loath to let go,
they are so cool, so drunk with
the swirl of the wind and of the river—
oblivious to winter,
the last to let go and fall
into the water and on the ground.

To Waken an Old Lady

Old age is
a flight of small
cheeping birds
skimming
bare trees
above a snow glaze.
Gaining and failing
they are buffeted
by a dark wind—
But what?
On harsh weedstalks
the flock has rested—
the snow
is covered with broken
seedhusks
and the wind tempered
with a shrill
piping of plenty.

The Great Figure

Among the rain
and lights
I saw the figure 5
in gold

on a red
firetruck
moving
tense
unheeded
to gong clangs
siren howls
and wheels rumbling
through the dark city.

HUMBERT WOLFE
(1885–1940)

Thrushes

The City Financier
walks in the Gardens
stiffly, because of
his pride and his burdens.

The daisies looking
up, observe,
only a self-
respecting curve.

The thrushes only
see a flat
table-land
of shiny hat.

He looks importantly
about him,
while all the spring
goes on without him.

The Lilac

Who thought of the lilac?
"I," dew said.
"I made up the lilac
out of my head."

"She made up the lilac!
Pooh!" thrilled a linnet,
and each dew-note had a
lilac in it.

ELINOR WYLIE
(1885–1928)

Beauty

Say not of Beauty she is good,
Or aught but beautiful,
Or sleek to doves' wings of the wood
Her wild wings of a gull.

Call her not wicked; that word's touch
Consumes her like a curse;
But love her not too much, too much,
For that is even worse.

O, she is neither good nor bad,
But innocent and wild!
Enshrine her and she dies, who had
The hard heart of a child.

WILLIAM BUTLER YEATS
(1865–1939)

A Drinking Song

Wine comes in at the mouth
And love comes in at the eye;
That's all we shall know for truth
Before we grow old and die.
I lift the glass to my mouth,
I look at you, and I sigh.

The Lover Pleads with His Friend for Old Friends

Though you are in your shining days,
Voices among the crowd
And new friends busy with your praise,
Be not unkind or proud,   ·
But think about old friends the most:
Time's bitter flood will rise,
Your beauty perish and be lost
For all eyes but these eyes.

A Deep-sworn Vow

Others because you did not keep
That deep-sworn vow have been friends of mine;
Yet always when I look death in the face,
When I clamber to the heights of sleep,
Or when I grow excited with wine,
Suddenly I meet your face.

He Wishes for the Cloths of Heaven

Had I the heavens' embroidered cloths,
Enwrought with the golden and silver light,
The blue and the dim and the dark cloths
Of night and light and the half light,
I would spread the cloths under your feet:
But I, being poor, have only my dreams;
I have spread my dreams beneath your feet;
Tread softly because you tread on my dreams.

YEVGENY YEVTUSHENKO
(b. 1933)

Knock at the Door

'Who is it?'
        'Age,
                coming for you.'
'Come later on.
        Too busy.
                Things to do.'
To write
        To telephone
                eat an omelette.
No one was waiting when I opened up.
Was it a joke?
        Did I get
                the name wrong?
Can it have been
        maturity
                that came
and sighed
        and wouldn't wait
                and has gone?

Alphabetical List of Titles and First Lines

Titles are given in italics only when distinct from the first lines.

~

A CATALOG OF SELECTED
DOVER BOOKS
IN ALL FIELDS OF INTEREST

A CATALOG OF SELECTED DOVER
BOOKS IN ALL FIELDS OF INTEREST

100 BEST-LOVED POEMS, Edited by Philip Smith. "The Passionate Shepherd to His Love," "Shall I compare thee to a summer's day?" "Death, be not proud," "The Raven," "The Road Not Taken," plus works by Blake, Wordsworth, Byron, Shelley, Keats, many others. 96pp. 5³⁄₁₆ x 8¼.   0-486-28553-7

100 SMALL HOUSES OF THE THIRTIES, Brown-Blodgett Company. Exterior photographs and floor plans for 100 charming structures. Illustrations of models accompanied by descriptions of interiors, color schemes, closet space, and other amenities. 200 illustrations. 112pp. 8⅜ x 11.   0-486-44131-8

1000 TURN-OF-THE-CENTURY HOUSES: With Illustrations and Floor Plans, Herbert C. Chivers. Reproduced from a rare edition, this showcase of homes ranges from cottages and bungalows to sprawling mansions. Each house is meticulously illustrated and accompanied by complete floor plans. 256pp. 9⅜ x 12¼.

     0-486-45596-3

101 GREAT AMERICAN POEMS, Edited by The American Poetry & Literacy Project. Rich treasury of verse from the 19th and 20th centuries includes works by Edgar Allan Poe, Robert Frost, Walt Whitman, Langston Hughes, Emily Dickinson, T. S. Eliot, other notables. 96pp. 5³⁄₁₆ x 8¼.   0-486-40158-8

101 GREAT SAMURAI PRINTS, Utagawa Kuniyoshi. Kuniyoshi was a master of the warrior woodblock print — and these 18th-century illustrations represent the pinnacle of his craft. Full-color portraits of renowned Japanese samurais pulse with movement, passion, and remarkably fine detail. 112pp. 8⅜ x 11.   0-486-46523-3

ABC OF BALLET, Janet Grosser. Clearly worded, abundantly illustrated little guide defines basic ballet-related terms: arabesque, battement, pas de chat, relevé, sissonne, many others. Pronunciation guide included. Excellent primer. 48pp. 4³⁄₁₆ x 5¾.

     0-486-40871-X

ACCESSORIES OF DRESS: An Illustrated Encyclopedia, Katherine Lester and Bess Viola Oerke. Illustrations of hats, veils, wigs, cravats, shawls, shoes, gloves, and other accessories enhance an engaging commentary that reveals the humor and charm of the many-sided story of accessorized apparel. 644 figures and 59 plates. 608pp. 6⅛ x 9¼.

     0-486-43378-1

ADVENTURES OF HUCKLEBERRY FINN, Mark Twain. Join Huck and Jim as their boyhood adventures along the Mississippi River lead them into a world of excitement, danger, and self-discovery. Humorous narrative, lyrical descriptions of the Mississippi valley, and memorable characters. 224pp. 5³⁄₁₆ x 8¼.   0-486-28061-6

ALICE STARMORE'S BOOK OF FAIR ISLE KNITTING, Alice Starmore. A noted designer from the region of Scotland's Fair Isle explores the history and techniques of this distinctive, stranded-color knitting style and provides copious illustrated instructions for 14 original knitwear designs. 208pp. 8⅜ x 10⅞.   0-486-47218-3

Browse over 9,000 books at www.doverpublications.com

CATALOG OF DOVER BOOKS

ALICE'S ADVENTURES IN WONDERLAND, Lewis Carroll. Beloved classic about a little girl lost in a topsy-turvy land and her encounters with the White Rabbit, March Hare, Mad Hatter, Cheshire Cat, and other delightfully improbable characters. 42 illustrations by Sir John Tenniel. 96pp. 5³⁄₁₆ x 8¼. 0-486-27543-4

AMERICA'S LIGHTHOUSES: An Illustrated History, Francis Ross Holland. Profusely illustrated fact-filled survey of American lighthouses since 1716. Over 200 stations — East, Gulf, and West coasts, Great Lakes, Hawaii, Alaska, Puerto Rico, the Virgin Islands, and the Mississippi and St. Lawrence Rivers. 240pp. 8 x 10¾.
0-486-25576-X

AN ENCYCLOPEDIA OF THE VIOLIN, Alberto Bachmann. Translated by Frederick H. Martens. Introduction by Eugene Ysaye. First published in 1925, this renowned reference remains unsurpassed as a source of essential information, from construction and evolution to repertoire and technique. Includes a glossary and 73 illustrations. 496pp. 6⅛ x 9¼. 0-486-46618-3

ANIMALS: 1,419 Copyright-Free Illustrations of Mammals, Birds, Fish, Insects, etc., Selected by Jim Harter. Selected for its visual impact and ease of use, this outstanding collection of wood engravings presents over 1,000 species of animals in extremely lifelike poses. Includes mammals, birds, reptiles, amphibians, fish, insects, and other invertebrates. 284pp. 9 x 12. 0-486-23766-4

THE ANNALS, Tacitus. Translated by Alfred John Church and William Jackson Brodribb. This vital chronicle of Imperial Rome, written by the era's great historian, spans A.D. 14-68 and paints incisive psychological portraits of major figures, from Tiberius to Nero. 416pp. 5³⁄₁₆ x 8¼. 0-486-45236-0

ANTIGONE, Sophocles. Filled with passionate speeches and sensitive probing of moral and philosophical issues, this powerful and often-performed Greek drama reveals the grim fate that befalls the children of Oedipus. Footnotes. 64pp. 5³⁄₁₆ x 8 ¼. 0-486-27804-2

ART DECO DECORATIVE PATTERNS IN FULL COLOR, Christian Stoll. Reprinted from a rare 1910 portfolio, 160 sensuous and exotic images depict a breathtaking array of florals, geometrics, and abstracts — all elegant in their stark simplicity. 64pp. 8⅜ x 11. 0-486-44862-2

THE ARTHUR RACKHAM TREASURY: 86 Full-Color Illustrations, Arthur Rackham. Selected and Edited by Jeff A. Menges. A stunning treasury of 86 full-page plates span the famed English artist's career, from *Rip Van Winkle* (1905) to masterworks such as *Undine, A Midsummer Night's Dream,* and *Wind in the Willows* (1939). 96pp. 8⅜ x 11.
0-486-44685-9

THE AUTHENTIC GILBERT & SULLIVAN SONGBOOK, W. S. Gilbert and A. S. Sullivan. The most comprehensive collection available, this songbook includes selections from every one of Gilbert and Sullivan's light operas. Ninety-two numbers are presented uncut and unedited, and in their original keys. 410pp. 9 x 12.
0-486-23482-7

THE AWAKENING, Kate Chopin. First published in 1899, this controversial novel of a New Orleans wife's search for love outside a stifling marriage shocked readers. Today, it remains a first-rate narrative with superb characterization. New introductory Note. 128pp. 5³⁄₁₆ x 8¼. 0-486-27786-0

BASIC DRAWING, Louis Priscilla. Beginning with perspective, this commonsense manual progresses to the figure in movement, light and shade, anatomy, drapery, composition, trees and landscape, and outdoor sketching. Black-and-white illustrations throughout. 128pp. 8⅜ x 11. 0-486-45815-6

Browse over 9,000 books at www.doverpublications.com

THE BATTLES THAT CHANGED HISTORY, Fletcher Pratt. Historian profiles 16 crucial conflicts, ancient to modern, that changed the course of Western civilization. Gripping accounts of battles led by Alexander the Great, Joan of Arc, Ulysses S. Grant, other commanders. 27 maps. 352pp. 5⅜ x 8½.   0-486-41129-X

BEETHOVEN'S LETTERS, Ludwig van Beethoven. Edited by Dr. A. C. Kalischer. Features 457 letters to fellow musicians, friends, greats, patrons, and literary men. Reveals musical thoughts, quirks of personality, insights, and daily events. Includes 15 plates. 410pp. 5⅜ x 8½.   0-486-22769-3

BERNICE BOBS HER HAIR AND OTHER STORIES, F. Scott Fitzgerald. This brilliant anthology includes 6 of Fitzgerald's most popular stories: "The Diamond as Big as the Ritz," the title tale, "The Offshore Pirate," "The Ice Palace," "The Jelly Bean," and "May Day." 176pp. 5⅜ x 8½.   0-486-47049-0

BESLER'S BOOK OF FLOWERS AND PLANTS: 73 Full-Color Plates from Hortus Eystettensis, 1613, Basilius Besler. Here is a selection of magnificent plates from the *Hortus Eystettensis,* which vividly illustrated and identified the plants, flowers, and trees that thrived in the legendary German garden at Eichstätt. 80pp. 8⅜ x 11.
        0-486-46005-3

THE BOOK OF KELLS, Edited by Blanche Cirker. Painstakingly reproduced from a rare facsimile edition, this volume contains full-page decorations, portraits, illustrations, plus a sampling of textual leaves with exquisite calligraphy and ornamentation. 32 full-color illustrations. 32pp. 9⅜ x 12¼.   0-486-24345-1

THE BOOK OF THE CROSSBOW: With an Additional Section on Catapults and Other Siege Engines, Ralph Payne-Gallwey. Fascinating study traces history and use of crossbow as military and sporting weapon, from Middle Ages to modern times. Also covers related weapons: balistas, catapults, Turkish bows, more. Over 240 illustrations. 400pp. 7¼ x 10⅛.   0-486-28720-3

THE BUNGALOW BOOK: Floor Plans and Photos of 112 Houses, 1910, Henry L. Wilson. Here are 112 of the most popular and economic blueprints of the early 20th century — plus an illustration or photograph of each completed house. A wonderful time capsule that still offers a wealth of valuable insights. 160pp. 8⅜ x 11.
        0-486-45104-6

THE CALL OF THE WILD, Jack London. A classic novel of adventure, drawn from London's own experiences as a Klondike adventurer, relating the story of a heroic dog caught in the brutal life of the Alaska Gold Rush. Note. 64pp. 5³⁄₁₆ x 8¼.
        0-486-26472-6

CANDIDE, Voltaire. Edited by Francois-Marie Arouet. One of the world's great satires since its first publication in 1759. Witty, caustic skewering of romance, science, philosophy, religion, government — nearly all human ideals and institutions. 112pp. 5³⁄₁₆ x 8¼.   0-486-26689-3

CELEBRATED IN THEIR TIME: Photographic Portraits from the George Grantham Bain Collection, Edited by Amy Pastan. With an Introduction by Michael Carlebach. Remarkable portrait gallery features 112 rare images of Albert Einstein, Charlie Chaplin, the Wright Brothers, Henry Ford, and other luminaries from the worlds of politics, art, entertainment, and industry. 128pp. 8⅜ x 11.   0-486-46754-6

CHARIOTS FOR APOLLO: The NASA History of Manned Lunar Spacecraft to 1969, Courtney G. Brooks, James M. Grimwood, and Loyd S. Swenson, Jr. This illustrated history by a trio of experts is the definitive reference on the Apollo spacecraft and lunar modules. It traces the vehicles' design, development, and operation in space. More than 100 photographs and illustrations. 576pp. 6¾ x 9¼. 0-486-46756-2

Browse over 9,000 books at www.doverpublications.com

A CHRISTMAS CAROL, Charles Dickens. This engrossing tale relates Ebenezer Scrooge's ghostly journeys through Christmases past, present, and future and his ultimate transformation from a harsh and grasping old miser to a charitable and compassionate human being. 80pp. 5³⁄₁₆ x 8¼. 0-486-26865-9

COMMON SENSE, Thomas Paine. First published in January of 1776, this highly influential landmark document clearly and persuasively argued for American separation from Great Britain and paved the way for the Declaration of Independence. 64pp. 5³⁄₁₆ x 8¼. 0-486-29602-4

THE COMPLETE SHORT STORIES OF OSCAR WILDE, Oscar Wilde. Complete texts of "The Happy Prince and Other Tales," "A House of Pomegranates," "Lord Arthur Savile's Crime and Other Stories," "Poems in Prose," and "The Portrait of Mr. W. H." 208pp. 5³⁄₁₆ x 8¼. 0-486-45216-6

COMPLETE SONNETS, William Shakespeare. Over 150 exquisite poems deal with love, friendship, the tyranny of time, beauty's evanescence, death, and other themes in language of remarkable power, precision, and beauty. Glossary of archaic terms. 80pp. 5³⁄₁₆ x 8¼. 0-486-26686-9

THE COUNT OF MONTE CRISTO: Abridged Edition, Alexandre Dumas. Falsely accused of treason, Edmond Dantès is imprisoned in the bleak Chateau d'If. After a hair-raising escape, he launches an elaborate plot to extract a bitter revenge against those who betrayed him. 448pp. 5³⁄₁₆ x 8¼. 0-486-45643-9

CRAFTSMAN BUNGALOWS: Designs from the Pacific Northwest, Yoho & Merritt. This reprint of a rare catalog, showcasing the charming simplicity and cozy style of Craftsman bungalows, is filled with photos of completed homes, plus floor plans and estimated costs. An indispensable resource for architects, historians, and illustrators. 112pp. 10 x 7. 0-486-46875-5

CRAFTSMAN BUNGALOWS: 59 Homes from "The Craftsman," Edited by Gustav Stickley. Best and most attractive designs from Arts and Crafts Movement publication — 1903–1916 — includes sketches, photographs of homes, floor plans, descriptive text. 128pp. 8¼ x 11. 0-486-25829-7

CRIME AND PUNISHMENT, Fyodor Dostoyevsky. Translated by Constance Garnett. Supreme masterpiece tells the story of Raskolnikov, a student tormented by his own thoughts after he murders an old woman. Overwhelmed by guilt and terror, he confesses and goes to prison. 480pp. 5³⁄₁₆ x 8¼. 0-486-41587-2

THE DECLARATION OF INDEPENDENCE AND OTHER GREAT DOCUMENTS OF AMERICAN HISTORY: 1775-1865, Edited by John Grafton. Thirteen compelling and influential documents: Henry's "Give Me Liberty or Give Me Death," Declaration of Independence, The Constitution, Washington's First Inaugural Address, The Monroe Doctrine, The Emancipation Proclamation, Gettysburg Address, more. 64pp. 5³⁄₁₆ x 8¼. 0-486-41124-9

THE DESERT AND THE SOWN: Travels in Palestine and Syria, Gertrude Bell. "The female Lawrence of Arabia," Gertrude Bell wrote captivating, perceptive accounts of her travels in the Middle East. This intriguing narrative, accompanied by 160 photos, traces her 1905 sojourn in Lebanon, Syria, and Palestine. 368pp. 5⅜ x 8½.
0-486-46876-3

A DOLL'S HOUSE, Henrik Ibsen. Ibsen's best-known play displays his genius for realistic prose drama. An expression of women's rights, the play climaxes when the central character, Nora, rejects a smothering marriage and life in "a doll's house." 80pp. 5³⁄₁₆ x 8¼. 0-486-27062-9

DOOMED SHIPS: Great Ocean Liner Disasters, William H. Miller, Jr. Nearly 200 photographs, many from private collections, highlight tales of some of the vessels whose pleasure cruises ended in catastrophe: the *Morro Castle, Normandie, Andrea Doria, Europa,* and many others. 128pp. 8⅞ x 11¾. 0-486-45366-9

THE DORÉ BIBLE ILLUSTRATIONS, Gustave Doré. Detailed plates from the Bible: the Creation scenes, Adam and Eve, horrifying visions of the Flood, the battle sequences with their monumental crowds, depictions of the life of Jesus, 241 plates in all. 241pp. 9 x 12. 0-486-23004-X

DRAWING DRAPERY FROM HEAD TO TOE, Cliff Young. Expert guidance on how to draw shirts, pants, skirts, gloves, hats, and coats on the human figure, including folds in relation to the body, pull and crush, action folds, creases, more. Over 200 drawings. 48pp. 8¼ x 11. 0-486-45591-2

DUBLINERS, James Joyce. A fine and accessible introduction to the work of one of the 20th century's most influential writers, this collection features 15 tales, including a masterpiece of the short-story genre, "The Dead." 160pp. 5³⁄₁₆ x 8¼.
0-486-26870-5

EASY-TO-MAKE POP-UPS, Joan Irvine. Illustrated by Barbara Reid. Dozens of wonderful ideas for three-dimensional paper fun — from holiday greeting cards with moving parts to a pop-up menagerie. Easy-to-follow, illustrated instructions for more than 30 projects. 299 black-and-white illustrations. 96pp. 8⅜ x 11.
0-486-44622-0

EASY-TO-MAKE STORYBOOK DOLLS: A "Novel" Approach to Cloth Dollmaking, Sherralyn St. Clair. Favorite fictional characters come alive in this unique beginner's dollmaking guide. Includes patterns for Pollyanna, Dorothy from *The Wonderful Wizard of Oz,* Mary of *The Secret Garden,* plus easy-to-follow instructions, 263 black-and-white illustrations, and an 8-page color insert. 112pp. 8¼ x 11. 0-486-47360-0

EINSTEIN'S ESSAYS IN SCIENCE, Albert Einstein. Speeches and essays in accessible, everyday language profile influential physicists such as Niels Bohr and Isaac Newton. They also explore areas of physics to which the author made major contributions. 128pp. 5 x 8. 0-486-47011-3

EL DORADO: Further Adventures of the Scarlet Pimpernel, Baroness Orczy. A popular sequel to *The Scarlet Pimpernel,* this suspenseful story recounts the Pimpernel's attempts to rescue the Dauphin from imprisonment during the French Revolution. An irresistible blend of intrigue, period detail, and vibrant characterizations. 352pp. 5³⁄₁₆ x 8¼. 0-486-44026-5

ELEGANT SMALL HOMES OF THE TWENTIES: 99 Designs from a Competition, Chicago Tribune. Nearly 100 designs for five- and six-room houses feature New England and Southern colonials, Normandy cottages, stately Italianate dwellings, and other fascinating snapshots of American domestic architecture of the 1920s. 112pp. 9 x 12. 0-486-46910-7

THE ELEMENTS OF STYLE: The Original Edition, William Strunk, Jr. This is the book that generations of writers have relied upon for timeless advice on grammar, diction, syntax, and other essentials. In concise terms, it identifies the principal requirements of proper style and common errors. 64pp. 5⅜ x 8½. 0-486-44798-7

THE ELUSIVE PIMPERNEL, Baroness Orczy. Robespierre's revolutionaries find their wicked schemes thwarted by the heroic Pimpernel — Sir Percival Blakeney. In this thrilling sequel, Chauvelin devises a plot to eliminate the Pimpernel and his wife. 272pp. 5³⁄₁₆ x 8¼. 0-486-45464-9

Browse over 9,000 books at www.doverpublications.com